"This wonderful book will take you on a fascinating and sure-footed journey through the real world of crime scene investigation and the real people in it. *Bodies We've Buried* is original, informative, and delightfully readable."
—Patricia Cornwell

"A fascinating inside look...The Academy's rigorous, hands-on curriculum is not for the faint of heart or the queasy. The same could be said for the book's vivid you-are-there descriptions...People looking for an interesting read will enjoy sharing the challenges of the CSI training course and the behind-the-scenes stories that Hallcox and Welch recount. Their enthusiastic and comfortable style welcomes all readers, viewers and nonviewers of *CSI* alike, into their world."
—Dr. Fred Bortz, *Chicago Sun-Times*

"Hallcox and Welch take readers inside the world's top CSI training school for a spooky, but fascinating, look at what they do and how they do it."
—*The Knoxville News-Sentinel*

"More gruesome than anything on *CSI*."
—*Giant*

"It isn't pretty, but exposure to such disturbing sights and smells helps detectives track down the bad guys."
—*Nashville Scene*

"Shares with readers the gritty reality of forensic work. The authors caution that the actual work is a lot less glamorous than it looks on TV and often involves crawling through the mud or examining putrid corpses. And nothing is as simple as it seems, from photographing crime scenes—where the details, from film speed to lighting, are crucial—to processing evidence, which is selectively sent off to a state lab to be dealt with. Students in the course also pay a visit to the infamous Body Farm, where they examine and analyze decomposing corpses. Given the popularity of *CSI* and its many imitators, many will find reading about the real science enlightening and engrossing."
—*Booklist*

Berkley titles by
Jarrett Hallcox and Amy Welch

BODIES WE'VE BURIED

BEHIND THE YELLOW TAPE

BEHIND THE YELLOW TAPE

On the Road with Some of America's

Hardest Working

Crime Scene Investigators

JARRETT HALLCOX and AMY WELCH

BERKLEY BOOKS, NEW YORK

THE BERKLEY PUBLISHING GROUP
Published by the Penguin Group
Penguin Group (USA) Inc.
375 Hudson Street, New York, New York 10014, USA
Penguin Group (Canada), 90 Eglinton Avenue East, Suite 700, Toronto, Ontario M4P 2Y3, Canada
(a division of Pearson Penguin Canada Inc.)
Penguin Books Ltd., 80 Strand, London WC2R 0RL, England
Penguin Group Ireland, 25 St. Stephen's Green, Dublin 2, Ireland (a division of Penguin Books Ltd.)
Penguin Group (Australia), 250 Camberwell Road, Camberwell, Victoria 3124, Australia
(a division of Pearson Australia Group Pty. Ltd.)
Penguin Books India Pvt. Ltd., 11 Community Centre, Panchsheel Park, New Delhi—110 017, India
Penguin Group (NZ), 67 Apollo Drive, Rosedale, North Shore 0632, New Zealand
(a division of Pearson New Zealand Ltd.)
Penguin Books (South Africa) (Pty.) Ltd., 24 Sturdee Avenue, Rosebank, Johannesburg 2196,
South Africa

Penguin Books Ltd., Registered Offices: 80 Strand, London WC2R 0RL, England

This book is an original publication of The Berkley Publishing Group.

The publisher does not have any control over and does not assume any responsibility for author or
third-party websites or their content.

PRINTING HISTORY
Berkley trade paperback edition / January 2009

Library of Congress Cataloging-in-Publication Data

Hallcox, Jarrett.
    Behind the yellow tape : on the road with some of America's hardest working crime scene
investigators / Jarrett Hallcox and Amy Welch ; foreword by Patricia Cornwell.
       p. cm.
    ISBN 978-0-425-22166-2 (pbk.)
    1. Criminal investigation—United States—Case studies.   2. Crime scene searches—
United States—Case studies.   3. Evidence, Criminal—United States—Case studies.
I. Welch, Amy.   II. Title.
    HV8073.H2228 2009
    363.25092'273—dc22

                                                                                    2008035648

PRINTED IN THE UNITED STATES OF AMERICA

10   9   8   7   6   5   4   3   2   1

*To all who have dedicated their lives
to forensic science and work tirelessly to stay
one step ahead of the criminal.*

CONTENTS

Only those who will risk going too far
can possibly find out how far one can go.
—T. S. ELIOT

FOREWORD

BY PATRICIA CORNWELL

There's always evidence, if you know where to look. So we realize in *Behind the Yellow Tape*, a collection of real cases worked by real people who aren't likely to end up on talk shows, and probably won't like all the fuss when the public gets its hands on this tremendously entertaining, provocative book.

Behind the Yellow Tape isn't at all what you see on TV. It's better. It isn't done with *magic boxes*, as I refer to the television tools of CSIs, with their unlimited funding, limitless boundaries, and the ability to divine what happened and why. Jarrett Hallcox and Amy Welch trekked across America, spending countless hours with police and investigators as diverse as the sheriff's department of Sevier County, Tennessee, and the NYPD. As forensic experts themselves, who have each earned a ticket to the inside, the authors were given access to cases that they have re-created in such colorful, extraordinary detail, I got nervous and felt compelled to call Jarrett Hallcox after I'd read the first ten pages.

"Hey," I said uneasily, because he'd asked if I'd write a foreword to the book, and I was beginning to think I should have said no. "I'm confused. Is this fiction or nonfiction?"

"What do you mean?" he replied, baffled.

"I mean is it factual? Every word of it."

"Yes. Every word of it, I swear."

"Because I can't put my name on it and then find out later you made it up. What they call nonfiction-fiction or whatever," I said. "That's what it reads like. How the hell did you get all this detail, right down to what was said at the scene or what was going on inside someone's psyche?"

Painstaking research is the simple answer. Spending inordinate amounts of time talking to the cops who worked the cases, and going over every word of every record and interview. What comes to mind is an old saying I hear all the time from people who work in the world of crime: "You really can't make stuff like this up."

Of course, the big bonus is that Hallcox and Welch go to great lengths accurately describing the minutiae of forensics that no one can seem to get enough of these days. What you'll see is the very necessary demythologizing of crime scene investigation—what was and wasn't done in cases that shed blood and took lives.

INTRODUCTION
On the Road

What exactly is a crime scene investigator? Not the high-heeled, leather-clad version that Hollywood crams down our throats on a nightly basis, but the *real* crime scene investigator: the real CSI. Though there are no strict definitions, a crime scene investigator is simply a member of the police force who works a crime scene. Contrary to their name, they don't actually investigate crime—though some do have the dual responsibility of crime scene work and investigation. And they are not scientists either, unlike the character on *CSI*, Gil Grissom, who is shown toiling hours and hours in a laboratory. Simply put, CSIs are the people who collect evidence, do minimal analysis of that evidence, and prepare the rest to be sent to the lab. That's it. They don't use scanning electron microscopes, and they don't chase down murderers in long, dark alleyways. Hollywood purposefully gets it wrong, because sometimes being a CSI is boring. Crawling on your hands and knees, decked out in blaring white Tyvek suits, looking for one spent shell casing in the grass, or better still, sorting through a Dumpster behind an old Chinese restaurant, looking for a hair in day-old moo goo gai pan just doesn't make for a good prime-time broadcast.

Yet Hollywood's version has created a forensic fervor of epidemic proportions. The CSI craze has taken off, run amok, and left an indelible mark on pop culture. Hollywood's contribution to making crime scene investigation fashionable and "hot" cannot be denied. Just go to any college campus with a forensic science program and you will see it packed to the gills. The study of forensics is at its zenith, and Hollywood can be thanked for that. But unfortunately it has also had a negative impact as well. Shows such as *CSI* and *Cold Case* have caused some of the general public to have unreasonable expectations regarding crime scene investigation, due in large part to the sensational portrayal of crime scene investigators and their crime scene practices. And all of this has caused a new illness to develop, afflicting many, many Americans. It is called the *CSI Effect*.

The CSI Effect is a clear indicator of just how pervasive the forensic craze is. Smart, intelligent people are watching these forensic shows on television and thinking that they are true representations of crime and crime scene investigation. Some of these same people, armed with this silicone-enhanced knowledge of forensic science, end up as jurors who make their decisions based on what they have seen on TV and render verdicts based on what they think they know. "I saw it on television" has become an all-too-familiar response in courtrooms across America. It doesn't matter the size of the city or the type of crime; the CSI Effect does not discriminate. If you don't think the CSI Effect is a problem, just ask any forensic investigator who has testified at a hearing. We guarantee he or she will have a story to tell.

Why does any of this matter? Who cares, right? Wrong. It matters because the crime scene investigator is the first line in seeking justice. In most criminal cases, the burden of proof comes down to the evidence—no more, no less. If the CSI does not find the evidence, collect it, and package it properly, then a trial won't even happen. There may not even be an arrest. The fate of a criminal begins and ends with the crime scene investigator and his or her ability to work a crime scene.

That's where we come in. We have spent the last six years of our lives working with and training crime scene investigators at the National Forensic Academy (NFA) in Knoxville, Tennessee. Here, men and women from all walks of life and all types of law enforcement agencies come together to hone their CSI skills in an intense, hands-on training program unlike any other in the country. Three times a year and for ten weeks at a time, these CSIs train in the field via re-created crime scene scenarios. Cars are blown up, bodies are buried, and human blood is spattered in an effort to teach CSIs the best methods for working crime scenes. It is from here that benchmarks in the art of crime scene investigation are set, and it is from here that we, former administrators of this renowned academy, learned the real world of crime scene investigation and the trials, tribulations, and triumphs of the crime scene investigator.

So we decided to tell their stories; to walk a mile in their shoes; and hopefully, just maybe, to debunk some of the Hollywood myths surrounding the CSI. Not to mention, we wanted to give CSIs everywhere their due because, contrary to how they are portrayed on television, their jobs are not glamorous, high paying, or even particularly rewarding at times. They don't have the corner offices or the high-tech labs—and you can rest assured none of them drive Hummers. Sometimes television has a way of blurring the lines between what is real and what is make-believe. But we know what's real. It is these men and women, from border to border and coast to coast, who get up and go to work, laboring every single day to put bad people away, to make the rest of our lives better and safer. These are the stories of the men and women who dedicate their lives to working behind the yellow tape.

1

White Lightnin'

SEVIER COUNTY SHERIFF'S OFFICE, TENNESSEE

SEVIER COUNTY

TENNESSEE

Sevier County, Tennessee, sits in the heart of the Great Smoky Mountains. Founded in 1794, Sevier County was inhabited for more than fifteen thousand years by the Cherokee. The county was named after Tennessee's first governor, John Sevier. The county seat is Sevierville, one of the oldest cities in the entire state, though it's also home to other well-known cities—Gatlinburg and Pigeon Forge. Once dependent solely on farming, Sevier County is now home to major tourist attractions, including Great Smoky Mountains National Park and Dollywood, that keep the economy (and potential for crime) thriving. The Sevier County Sheriff's Office has eighty-nine employees. Seven of those are crime scene investigators.

Tucked into the foothills of the Great Smoky Mountains lies Sevier County, Tennessee, home to Dolly Parton, black bears, and a whole host of "good ol' boys" still making and runnin' shine—for medicinal purposes only, of course. Sevier County, in many ways, is a throwback to another era—a sort of crossroads between the twenty-first century and the antebellum South. It's not a major metropolitan area by any stretch of the imagination. There is no Watts or Bronx, in terms of dangerous urban neighborhoods, but that does not mean it is without crime or less-than-wholesome areas. Take, for instance, a place referred to as Frog Alley. Up until the late 1980s, cops could not patrol the area without being routinely trapped by local delinquents, armed to the gills with slingshots and buckets of ball bearings, lying in wait high up in the treetops for the cops to drive by. Flaming tires would be hurled at police cars as other tree-dwelling Frog Alleyans flung steel balls through windshields and car doors. Sometimes an officer's only defense was to jump out of the car with a shotgun and fire buckshot wildly into the treetops, just to be able to leave the area relatively unharmed. God only knows how many Frog Alleyans may have been hurt during those shootouts; in Frog Alley, they take care of their own.

But aside from the Frog Alley days, major disturbances are, for the most part, not a common thing in Sevier County. It is, above all else, a tourist area where people come by the tens of thousands in hopes of clean mountain air, funnel cakes, and sweet sorghum (it's like molasses—and sold on just about every roadside in the South). They have their fair share of shoot-'em-ups, meth labs, and the occasional "you-stole-my-woman" bar fights, mind you, but all in all, nothing too terribly violent tends to happen in this county. Rarely, if ever, are there any cases involving murderers who plan their kill and then bury the body. As a matter of fact, in the last twenty-five years, the Sevier County Sheriff's Office had never had a case involving a buried body. Then, on April 23, 2005, that streak came to an abrupt end.

Beautiful mountain vistas and clear valley streams surround the area known as English Mountain, Tennessee. English Mountain is an extraordinary sort of place. Back in the early 1970s it was intended to be a mountain getaway, where a wonderful community was being planned by some Ohioans with, as rumor has it, money made from selling cocaine. Trees were uprooted and a few crude roads were cut into the side of the mountain for this soon-to-be rural resort. But it was not to be.

Money got tight. Deeds were sold over and over and over again. They switched hands so many times that to this day, people are still in litigation over who actually owns some of the land. Since the 1970s, a few attempts have been made to revive this incredibly scenic (yet backward) place, but none have been successful. The "foreigners"—that is, anyone not born in Sevier County— were all run off by a local cavalcade of heathens known as the "Cosby Raiders." These boys, decked out in camouflage, waving the rebel flag, and driving their four-wheel-drive pickup trucks, would terrorize anyone who set foot on the mountain. As a result, no real residential settlement has ever developed. All that's left are approximately sixty mobile homes of varying upkeep spread throughout the mountainside, a small country grocery store, and a makeshift fire department.

The residents of English Mountain keep to themselves, leading fairly simple lives. Children run and play on small parcels of trailer park land, their bare feet smacking on the cold clay where grass used to grow. Adolescents run wild on the muddy mountain bluffs four-wheelin' in their ATVs, while the adults sit around in the evenings and talk, kicking rocks with the neighbors—a southern tradition.

Yet, as with most neighborhoods, English Mountain has its seedy side. Drugs are prevalent on the mountain, particularly marijuana and prescription pills. One person, known to many of the mountaineers simply as "Mountain Man," was renowned in the neighborhood as a primary source of these drugs. This Mountain Man, born with the name John Wayne

Blair, supplied several of his friends and neighbors with drugs, while they all partied hard together, hanging out in the woods or doing whatever they felt stoned enough or stupid enough to do. Two people in particular were regular subscribers to the Mountain Man's brand of medicine—Kelly Sellers and Tommy Humphries. The two of them, along with Blair, had a grand old time smoking dope and popping pills until one day, twenty-three-year-old Kelly Sellers went missing. From that day forward, English Mountain would never be the same.

A missing-person call came in to the sheriff's office from Kelly's frantic mother, who had not heard from her daughter in about twenty-four hours. Calls like this come in to the office all the time. Typically, it's just rebellious kids who have run off after a fight with their parents and come back in a day or two. Or, as investigators will attest, it is not uncommon for a resident of English Mountain to go on a two- or three-day drunken, dope-riddled orgy, then crawl back home late one evening. Whatever the case might have been, the sheriff's department dispatched Sergeant Michael Hodges to respond to the call. Sergeant Hodges is a colorful officer who can weave a tapestry of expletives to rival any bawdy comedian. He knew all too well that English Mountain had a whole host of lawbreakers and law skirters whom he and his fellow deputies had to deal with on a regular basis. Because of English Mountain's history, he didn't give much thought to this missing girl until he knocked on the door from where the call had originated. Kelly's mother was adamant, telling Sergeant Hodges that her daughter always called her to let her know what she was doing, even when what she was doing was not exactly church conversation. She knew her daughter partied, but Kelly *always* called home. She went on to tell Hodges that Kelly regularly hung out with Tommy Humphries and John Blair, the latter being, as far as she knew, the last person to be with Kelly before she went missing. Regardless of the information Kelly's mom gave him, Sergeant Hodges still didn't give the call much thought, but he promised that he would speak to both Humphries and Blair.

John Blair's residence was at the very end of Honeysuckle, one of the few paved roads on English Mountain. His domicile, a double-wide trailer, was set into the side of the mountain wall, sitting fairly far back off the road. When Sergeant Hodges approached the house, three vehicles were in the driveway, so he figured someone had to be home. As he stepped onto the porch, he noticed a sign taped to the front door that read: *I don't call 911, I aim my M16.* Upon reading that nice little warning note, he decided to unbutton his holster, just in case. He knocked, more than once, and even though he could hear someone stirring, no one came to the door. Without any tangible reason to press the issue at Blair's, he went back to Kelly's home to talk with her parents again.

This time, Kelly's mother began to get very accusatory toward Blair, explaining that he had recently become obsessed with Kelly, but her daughter wasn't interested in him "in that way"—especially considering that twenty-three-year-old Kelly was not only twenty-seven years his junior but a lesbian. Still,

The home of John Wayne Blair.
HALLCOX & WELCH, LLC

her mother told Sergeant Hodges, Blair had continued to proposition Kelly even though she kept turning him down. As the conversation unfolded and Kelly's mother grew ever more hysterical, another call came in from dispatch alerting Hodges that Blair's trailer was now reporting a fire. That meant it had caught fire during the brief time it had taken him to drive back to Kelly's mother, so Hodges rushed back up Honeysuckle to see "what the hell was going on."

Hodges slid to a halt at Blair's and jumped out of his cruiser, running toward the trailer. There was no sign of a fire, but out of the corner of his eye he caught a glimpse of a wiry old man with a dirty white beard. Lo and behold, it was

John Blair, perched on a bicycle no less. This was notably odd, since English Mountain is not prime real estate for cycling. Old rocky creek beds, mud dunes, and pig trails where wild boars roam are pretty much the sum total of the areas available for cycling.

English Mountain is a long way from the nearest fire department. However, a small volunteer fire department, housed in an old Quonset hut, is located down the road from Blair's house and just before the old grocery store. In the minutes that had passed since Hodges had first knocked on his door, Blair had ridden down to the store, ignoring the Quonset hut on his way, to telephone the fire department that his house was on fire. Then, inexplicably, he rode his bike back up the mountain to his house and ultimately put the fire out himself with a garden hose—all before Sergeant Hodges or the fire department had even arrived.

"If she's dead in the trailer, I want to know right fuckin' now," Hodges yelled to John Blair, who continued to sit on his bicycle outside his trailer as firefighters entered the house.

"Huh, I didn't hear you," Blair replied, unmoved at the events that were unfolding. Again Hodges vehemently asked Blair "if there was anybody in the house," and evidently hearing him this time, Blair simply replied, "Ain't nobody in that house, ain't nobody in there." Hodges ran through the house to make sure. While he was inside, Hodges noticed that only the bedroom had been burned; the rest of the house was fine. He found it unusual that only one room had caught fire. When he came out of the bedroom, one of the firemen told him, "I think we got some blood [on the floor]. I ain't sure. I ain't no expert, I'm a fireman." Hodges told him to cut a carpet sample, which he did and handed to Hodges, who carefully wrapped the sample in newspaper and put it in his trunk. Then he went back to Blair.

"Where have you been?" Hodges asked Blair. Hodges knew that something was just not right. His cop's intuition told him John Wayne Blair was up to no good.

"Riding my bike," Blair said, miffed, "that's what I's doin'."

Hodges proceeded to ask Blair when the last time was that he had seen Kelly Sellers. Blair began by railing about her being "crazy." "That's not what I asked you. When was the last time you saw Kelly?" repeated Hodges.

Defensive, Blair told Hodges that he had dropped her off at her parents' house "yesterday evening, around four or five." He went on to tell Hodges, "She's a dopehead; she eats pills."

"Well," Hodges started, "right now you're the last person that's seen her, and that's confirmed by her parents and you with the time frame you're giving me." But Blair stuck to his story, saying that they had just been talking and hanging out. While Hodges and Blair were conversing, Hodges noticed a fanny pack sitting on one of the cars near where they were standing. He asked Blair, for safety reasons, if he could see what was in the pack. Blair obligingly unzipped it and showed Hodges a roll of duct tape, condoms, a protein bar, and a knit cap. At that point, Hodges got into his car to make a note of the contents because "things weren't looking too good." But in all honesty, the evidence at that point was all circumstantial. There was still no substantive reason to think that anything had happened to Kelly, so Hodges left to find Tommy Humphries, the other individual who often hung out with Kelly Sellers and John Blair.

Humphries also lived on English Mountain, at the bottom of the hill, around the corner from the grocery store. Hodges had passed his house already and had noted that there were no vehicles in the driveway. But now, on his way back down from Blair's, he saw a truck in Humphries's yard and so he pulled in, hoping to have a conversation with Tommy. And, in fact, the moment Hodges's cruiser hit the driveway, Tommy hurriedly came out to talk, meeting him almost before Hodges was out of his car. Hodges asked what was going on. "You wouldn't be here if you didn't know," Humphries replied nervously. Hodges assured him that he did not, but he wanted to hear everything that Tommy knew. Humphries began to twitch, looking all around him as if something was bothering him. "I think somebody's got something aimed at me," he told Hodges uneasily. "Blair—he'll know I'm talking to you. He's probably got a scope on me right now!" Before Humphries went on with his story, he told Hodges that he had a gun in his back pocket.

"Do not move! Do not fuckin' move!" Hodges bellowed as he put his knee between Humphries's legs and removed the weapon from the man's back pocket. After clearing the weapon and putting it in his car, he told Humphries, "Okay, now we can talk."

"What I've got to say, you won't believe," Tommy went on to tell Hodges, "but I ain't telling you here." Humphries was worried about his children. "My babies are up the street at a friend's house. You get 'em off the mountain and then you and I can have a conversation." Hodges asked him if the conversation would end up in his having to call a mortuary. Humphries replied, "I guarantee it."

Hodges was now confronted with two people who intimately knew Kelly: one acting very suspicious and the other willing to spill his guts about what was starting to look more and more like a murder. Frankly, he didn't trust either of them, but he had to play the hand he was dealt. So Hodges assured Humphries that he would make sure his kids were safe and that he would ride with him back to the sheriff's office, where they would talk. After Hodges accompanied Humphries to the friend's house to check on the children, they left for the sheriff's office. Once they were far enough off the mountain for cell phone reception, Sergeant Hodges immediately phoned Detective Matt Cubberley in what was now the middle of the night.

Cubberley recalls, "I knew it was no lark when Hodges called and woke me up; when I arrived, Humphries and Hodges were both already back at the office." Cubberley is a big fellow (they call him "Box Head") who never shies away from the limelight. This case would turn out to be the biggest of his career. According to Cubberley, Humphries paced anxiously, not saying a word to anyone, traditionally the motions of a guilty man. He was awaiting news that his children had made it to their destination and were safely off the mountain. Once that call finally came in, Humphries spilled his guts, as if he had been holding back a flood.

"Party. That's what we do," he began. "Party, smoke dope, and ride four-wheelers." According to Humphries, the Friday before Kelly disappeared was supposed to be another day of the same—dope smoking and four-wheeling along with Blair. But Blair never called Humphries to make those plans. After waiting several hours, Tommy finally called John to see what was up. "I'm too tired to party," Blair told him over the phone. A very strange comment from a guy who was *never* too tired to party. Humphries said that Kelly was supposed to be there too, and he just assumed that Blair was "getting some" from her. So like any good partier, he simply went somewhere else on the mountain to smoke some dope.

The next day, Humphries and Blair had lunch at the local market and then drove back to John's trailer to hang out. As they stood in the driveway getting ready to go inside, Blair asked Humphries if he could keep a secret—a really big secret. And that's when he dropped the bomb. "I had to pop her." Before he could even ask why, Humphries claimed John said that "Kelly came to his house wanting pills and raising mortal hell, threatening to turn the whole fuckin' mountain in for selling dope if he did not give her some pills." Blair went on to give some details, saying that he had killed Kelly in his double-wide trailer and had buried her up on the mountain, right where a tree had fallen, using the upturned roots as the cover for her body. Humphries finished his story by telling the investigators he *had* noticed that Blair's house had smelled very strongly of bleach that morning.

. . .

We visited English Mountain on the one-year anniversary of Kelly Sellers's disappearance. The crime scene investigators who had worked the case had obtained a couple of all-terrain vehicles to transport all of us up the mountain, back to the scene of the crime. We convened with them at the English Mountain grocery store. For the CSIs who worked the case, this spot had been base camp for several days—the one small link between civilization and the English Mountain backcountry. Before heading out, Sergeant Hodges and the rest of the crew told war stories about recent experiences dealing with the criminal element in and around Sevier County. After keeping us in stitches for more than thirty minutes with a tale of a big ol' girl trying to "crunk" (that's Sevier Countyan for *crank*) her car with a straightedge screwdriver, we finally rolled our vehicles off the trailers and prepared for our ascent up the mountain.

As Detective Matt Cubberley told us, not knowing if Humphries was for real, he wasn't sure whether to arrest him. But his gut told him that Tommy was telling the truth, at least in part, and even if they eventually had to go after him as a

Sevier County Sheriff's Office, Tennessee, personnel: Jeff McCarter, Stephanie McClure, Matthew Cubberley, and Michael Hodges
HALLCOX & WELCH, LLC

co-conspirator, as it stood, the only evidence they had at all was what Humphries was telling them. For the moment, it was good enough.

"That's when I called in Stephanie and Jeff to help," Matt told us, as we stopped in front of Blair's house, the M16 warning still mocking us from the front door. Detective Jeff McCarter was in charge of processing the scene. He's the elder statesman of the group and, unlike Matt, avoids the media at all costs by scowling at everyone like a mad dog (though he's actually a big teddy bear whom his NFA classmates nicknamed "Buttercup"). Detective McCarter and Detective Stephanie McClure convened at the sheriff's office, where Matt caught them up to speed on what they had so far, ran priors on Blair, and had Humphries retell his story on tape so that Stephanie could write up a thorough and airtight search warrant—her specialty—for John Wayne Blair's house. Stephanie is the sugar of the CSI unit—the quintessential southern belle who looks and talks like Elly May Clampett. But don't let her charm fool you; she is as tough as nails and can cuss like a sailor. Once Jeff mapped in the coordinates to his GPS, we continued up one of the paths they thought might have been the one Blair took to dispose of Kelly's body.

"Blair had a prior conviction as a sex offender," Matt continued, as we bumped along the rocky terrain. Years earlier, while living in Florida, John Blair had kidnapped a girl, bound her with duct tape, and raped her. Ultimately he let her go and didn't kill her; she later testified against him at trial, and he served twelve years for his crimes. The detectives looked at each other, astonished, when they read the report. It seemed easy to imagine that Blair would've decided that letting the girl go had been a mistake—if he had killed her, she couldn't have testified against him, and he wouldn't have gone to prison. All signs indicated that he probably didn't make the same mistake twice.

• • •

With an airtight search warrant hot off the press, the three-person crime scene team gathered their supplies and drove to Blair's house in the wee hours of Sunday morning. Blair answered the door smug and confident and signed the consent-to-search form regardless of the warrant, giving them total access to the entire premises. The team had already determined that Stephanie and Matt would "good cop/bad cop" Blair while Jeff, the seasoned veteran, would work the crime scene.

Jeff had prepared for the task at hand by gathering equipment from their relatively new crime scene truck. After coming through the forensic studies program and realizing how far behind the Sevier County crime scene unit was in some areas, the investigators had formally requested new and better forensic supplies. They had needed to seriously upgrade their equipment, and happily they'd had the sheriff's complete support in doing so. They were able to procure the funds to buy and equip a fully stocked crime scene truck.

On his first of many trips to the truck, Jeff was told by one of the patrol officers that there wouldn't be any evidence to find because it had all burned up in the fire. Jeff, being a sly old dog, simply said, "There's always evidence, if you know where and how to look for it." The training that he'd received had taught him how to do just that.

Jeff began working the scene, culling through the bedroom that, oddly enough, didn't appear to contain a bed or any other kind of sleeping materials in it whatsoever. When Matt and Stephanie confronted Blair about that oddity, Blair simply claimed, "I always sleep on the couch." Back in the living room, Matt continued to interview John Blair, hoping for a confession. Stephanie went back and forth between the two areas, assisting Jeff in the bedroom and playing "good cop" when talking to Blair in the living room.

After several minutes of conversation, "bad cop" Matt got right to the point and called Blair a rapist to his face, agitating him, trying to do anything to get Blair to confess. At one point during the interview they even persuaded Blair to put his boots on and told him that they should all just go and find Kelly. But just before he seemed ready to get up and go outside with them, Blair became upset and called them sick bastards. "I did not kill her," he insisted. Up until that point, none of the investigators had said anything about her being dead, just missing—a point they made very clear to Blair.

Because the residence had paper-thin walls, Jeff could hear every word being said while he worked the scene. He would hear John Blair say something ludicrous and he would holler out, egging him on. "Keep talking, you son of a bitch; I'm finding all kinds of shit in here." But the evidence wasn't overwhelming. In the overly bleached-out and burned-out residence, the amount of evidence collected was minimal.

Jeff cut the carpet from the bedroom into square sections, methodically removing each one and checking on its underside. On the bottom of one section, he found what appeared to be a very small drop of blood, not much bigger than the end of a cotton swab. It was so small that he did not do a presumptive test to determine if it was blood on the carpet for fear of ruining the tiny sample for future analysis. He simply cut it out and collected it to send to the lab.

Normally in a case such as this, more than one CSI would be working the scene. But because Jeff's forte was evidence, he handled it by himself, walking from the crime scene truck to the bedroom, each time passing through the living room where Blair was being interrogated. On one of his trips from the truck, he came back into the trailer with a shovel and handed it to Blair. "Here, John, I've got another one just like it in the truck, let's you and me go dig her up." "You're a sick motherfucker," Blair responded. Jeff then said to Blair's face, "You let the first girl live and she told on you, so you killed this one so she couldn't." At that, Blair went berserk, cursing the CSI trio more and calling them all "sick bastards."

Jeff continued to work, finding blood in two other rooms of the house. A blood smear was found on a mop bucket inside the trailer alongside a ridiculous amount of cleaning supplies, including several empty bottles of a CSI's worst nightmare and a killer's best friend—bleach. A pair of Blair's rubber boots, which were sitting by the door, had tiny blood drops on them, and another small drop of blood was found on the door.

In one of the rooms in the mobile home, Jeff discovered a plethora of both large and small hand tools. Though not obviously connected to the crime scene, the presence of these assorted tools was unusual enough that Jeff took the time to log each and every serial number, in case any of them had been reported stolen. (Later, when he had someone back at the office run the serial numbers, none did turn out to have been reported; but then again, nobody trades a chain saw for pills and then reports it to the police.) With all of the evidence collected, the interior of the scene was complete. Jeff then turned his focus to processing Blair's truck for potential evidence. He had noticed earlier that Blair had recently pressure-washed the entire truck—so forcefully, in fact, that flecks of red paint were all over the ground where the pressure washer had torn them off. The vehicle had been cleaned from top to bottom, and Blair had clearly spent a lot of time on the truck bed, washing the water out the back with the tailgate down. But Jeff thoroughly worked the truck, and as spotless as the truck looked, he still found a tiny speck of blood on the underside of the tailgate—apparently the only place on the entire truck that Blair had missed.

Despite the blood evidence, it was still not enough to arrest Blair. Without sending the blood to a lab for analysis, they could not prove that the blood was Kelly Sellers's. Furthermore, it is not against the law to have a clean house, even one that does smell strongly of bleach; or a clean truck, even if it has been pressure-washed to hell; or even a bedroom without a bed. It's not even necessarily against the law to have a few drops of blood on the floor. Although it was certainly suspicious, all they knew for sure was that they had a missing adult and a few spots of blood in the house of the last person who had presumably seen her. So, without other options, after they had exhausted their search and interrogation, they reluctantly left Blair at his house and drove immediately down the road to Kelly's house to procure hair samples from a hairbrush in order to begin matching the DNA evidence. While they were there, they witnessed John Blair drive down the mountain in a little beater of a car. (He couldn't drive his truck because the assisting patrol officer had flattened his tires—an old trick to help slow down a suspect from fleeing the scene.) Frustrated, they couldn't do anything but watch Blair drive away. "There he goes," Jeff murmured to the others. "We'll never see that son of a bitch again."

The group was convinced that Kelly Sellers was dead, but they were not entirely sure of who had killed her or how many people may have been involved in her death. Nevertheless, they decided that the next thing they would do would be to search the mountain for her body. English Mountain is nothing more than thousands of acres of almost impassable land, with pig trails, creek beds, and hunting paths creating virtually the only access. The only clues the investigators had to go on were those given to them by Tommy Humphries, who was at best a questionable source, and who had provided only vague information about Kelly being buried near where a tree had fallen across a path. Probably thousands of places could fit that very description. With scavengers like wild pigs, raccoons, possums, and God only knows what else out on the mountain, plus the fact that the temperature was getting warmer, they needed to find her. The longer a body decomposes, the less physical evidence remains intact. Each hour is critical. Desperate, exhausted, and exasperated, the detectives decided to start the search first thing in the morning.

With the sun just breaking over the ridges of the mountains

the next morning, a call came in to the sheriff's office from an eyewitness stating that Tommy Humphries's house had been broken into and that guns had been stolen. The eyewitness named John Blair as the culprit. For some unknown reason, Blair had given Humphries his guns and then all of a sudden wanted them back. Come to find out, Blair had also given Humphries his four-wheeler. These gifts had been bestowed at around the same time as Kelly's disappearance. Why would Blair give Humphries all of that stuff? Was it in exchange for helping to dispose of a dead body?

. . .

Detective Mark Turner responded to the breaking-and-entering call at Tommy Humphries's house. Mark is a grizzled ex–narcotics investigator who, because of a near-death experience with pneumonia after getting lost while hunting in the mountains, now sounds like Larry the Cable Guy. He shares Larry's sense of humor too: the first day we met Mark, he had brought a mechanical hand that could remotely shoot us the bird, and he yelled Larry's catchphrase "Git 'er done" every chance he got. Unfortunately, Mark couldn't accompany us to revisit the scene because of some minor surgery he had undergone just two days before—so we "got 'er done" without him.

. . .

John Blair, now officially a wanted man, fled into the mountains— which left the investigators with a dilemma: an armed man, who they believed had already killed someone, was holed up on the very same mountain that they were searching for a dead body. It doesn't get much worse than that. Because of the dangers involved, no one was allowed to come in and help look for Kelly except the officers. It just wasn't safe—and the sheriff's office would be legally responsible if anyone got hurt. Detective Mark Turner, who'd gotten the arrest warrant for Blair, began the manhunt while Matt and Jeff went to gather the four-wheelers for the search.

One of the departments' four-wheelers was at another officer's house about twenty miles away from English Mountain. Jeff called to alert the officer that he was coming to get it. The officer, who worked as an SRO (School Resource Officer, a law enforcement officer assigned to a school system within that agency's jurisdiction) at the local high school, dashed home to have it ready and loaded onto the trailer when Jeff arrived. But when the officer arrived home, he could tell that something was not right. As soon as he rounded into his backyard, he noticed a pile of tools and other small equipment scattered on the ground beneath his back door. "Get over here fast," the officer yelled into his cell phone to Jeff. "Somebody's tried to break into my house!"

Jeff arrived within minutes to find, as reported, a slew of tools: chain saws, pressure washers, and more, just lying in the officer's backyard. There were no signs of an actual burglary, but strangely, none of the scattered tools and equipment belonged to the SRO either. But Jeff had no time at the moment to investigate this bizarre situation; with the rest of the sheriff's department stretched to the max, the odd case would have to wait. In the meantime, Jeff tossed the items into his truck, hooked up the trailer holding the four-wheeler, and sped back to the department, the missing Kelly Sellers weighing heavily on his mind.

If it hadn't been for needing to turn in the found items from the SRO's backyard, Jeff wouldn't even have gone back to the department; he would have gone straight to English Mountain to continue the search. But instead, he found himself hurriedly unloading all of the tools, mentally cataloging them as he brought them out: *Poulan Farmhand chain saw, Skil circular saw* ... He stopped dead in his tracks. "Poulan Farmhand chain saw," he said aloud. That brand of chain saw is uncommon, and Jeff had only ever seen one once before—at John Blair's house. Unbelievably, it appeared that all of the tools he had logged at Blair's had somehow made their way to the other officer's house. Was Blair sending a message to the sheriff's office? Was he toying with them?

Jeff dumped the tools at the office and rushed back up to Blair's, where several sheriff's deputies were already stationed. "You're not going to believe this," Jeff yelled to the group as he got out of his truck. "I just collected all of Blair's tools out from behind the SRO's house." As Jeff was unloading the four-wheeler, the deputies scratched their heads, and one of them stepped up to Jeff. "Hey, uh, I wanna show you some footprints over here," the officer said to Jeff. Jeff and the officer walked behind the trailer, away from everyone else, to look at the prints. But it was a ruse—there were none to be seen. The officer hesitated before admitting, "Uh, I heard another one of the officers talking about coming up here and getting those tools." Apparently, the other officer had been planning to steal the tools. "I want to know his fuckin' name!" Jeff yelled, for all of English Mountain to hear. The officer in question turned out to be one of the ones who had been assisting at Blair's on the night of the interrogation. Later in the day, after the tools had been discovered (but unbeknownst to the thief), the officer called the SRO to claim that he'd been kicked out of his storage unit and had left some tools behind his house for the afternoon. He'd be by later to pick them up. The SRO knew better, though, and angrily told the officer to call Jeff McCarter. The officer realized then that he was in trouble. His only response was, "Oh, shit!"

It was an appropriate response. He was immediately removed from the police force and ultimately pleaded guilty to the charge of aggravated burglary. He was made an example of and prosecuted to the fullest extent of the law, possibly serving as much as eight years, all for an old pressure washer and a used chain saw.

• • •

"I could have killed him," Jeff told us as we started down one of the dead-end trails he and Matt had taken over the course of a couple of days during the search. It's hard to imagine that anyone, especially an officer of the law, would be brazen or stupid enough to break into a presumed killer's house, especially one who was armed and desperate, in order to steal a couple of hundred dollars' worth of used tools. Not to mention jeopardize his career, let alone a potential capital murder case.

Later, when they finally caught Blair, the Mountain Man told them that he'd watched them, each and every one of them, as they searched over the four days and nights after he fled into the hills. He watched the officers go in and out of his house. At any time, he could have shot them with his rifle. Luckily, he wasn't that stupid. "What if he had shot and killed the officer when he went back for those tools?" Jeff pondered aloud to us. "We wouldn't have known what the hell had happened."

It's sad that Jeff, Matt, Stephanie, Mark, Michael, and all of the rest of the sheriff's department are now marked in Sevier County courts because of the actions of one dishonest officer. Regardless of the trial or the evidence that was collected, defense attorneys still take cheap shots at the sheriff's department whenever one of them is on the stand, calling them "crooked cops." All of this because one guy stole some used tools. The inflammatory statements cut like knives. All of the officers grew up in Sevier County, born and bred. And everyone in the county knows better than to think these officers would do such a thing. They deserve much better, but a defense attorney's job is to plant the seed of reasonable doubt, and no trick is too low for them to use to achieve that doubt. It's a shame, but one bad apple does spoil the whole bunch. When that officer's name comes up in court, they simply tell the jurors that they arrested him and prosecuted him—just as they would any other petty thief.

"That officer had balls, big uns," Jeff quipped, while stopping the vehicle and pointing to one of the hundreds of mounds of trash that dot English Mountain. Refrigerators, couches, full-size Tacoma truck beds, and entire Edsels and other miscellaneous cars from the 1950s and 1960s fill the ravines. The mountain adjoins another Tennessee County—Cocke County, notorious nationwide for the ability of some of its inhabitants to "chop" up a car in minutes. English Mountain is one of the locations where chop shops dispose of vehicle remains, tossing them to their final resting place at the bottom of the ravines. But that's not the only thing disposed of on the mountain. Trash pits dot the vast landscape, filled to the brim with all sorts of interesting items: refrigerators, old toys, couches, cribs, mattresses, box springs—you name it and it's there. Coincidentally, on the day Matt and Jeff were searching for Kelly, they happened upon the still-smoldering remains of a box spring, completely charred down to the metal springs. They had noted previously that Blair had recently removed the camper shell from his truck, as if to haul something large. Maybe he'd hauled off that bed he claimed to have never had? One year later, we could still see the remains of the box spring farther down in the trash heap.

We all climbed back into our ATVs, moving toward our final destination—the site where Kelly Sellers had been found.

Co-author Amy Welch looking at the remains of a burned mattress.
HALLCOX & WELCH, LLC

By now, more than four hours into our mountain adventure, our asses were beginning to ache. Jeff, an avid four-wheeler enthusiast, told us that he's raced around trails for eight hours or so, only to go home with his kidneys sore and pissing blood. Matt and Jeff ran all over the mountain for days. It might sound like fun, but it's not. It will absolutely wear you out.

. . .

With nothing more tangible to go on, they started their search for Kelly from the visible truck tracks leading away from Blair's house. Unfortunately, those tracks soon disappeared, mingling with the thousands of other hunting tracks that led in the same direction. At one point, they even brought Humphries on the trail with them, hoping he could show them where he and Blair had gone four-wheeling, thinking it might lead to where Kelly was buried. But after he led them all over the woods on tons of trails—and, for all they knew, on a wild-goose chase—they took him back and continued the search on their own. After hours and hours of searching, the two reluctantly stopped for the night, getting the only real sleep they had had in nearly seventy-two hours.

The next morning, a call came in to the sheriff's department with a potential lead, claiming that someone had seen Kelly in a Knoxville homeless shelter thirty miles away. Even though they knew it was probably erroneous, Detective Matt Cubberley had to check it out. Ultimately, as expected, a dead end, it made for a late start in the day's search for Kelly. Once they finally got back to the mountain, Detective Jeff McCarter, who had been all over the mountain hunting and four-wheeling numerous times before, decided to take a trail he was familiar with. By sheer happenstance, while on that trail they ran across another set of tracks that looked similar to those left around Blair's house. They followed the tracks until they reached a curve in the road that had a big dead tree lying across it, preventing them from going forward. They could tell by the tracks that a truck had stopped and made hesitation marks near the tree, but with nightfall looming and rain beginning to beat down on them, they were forced into another tough decision and had to leave the mountain while they still could. The paths were becoming treacherous as the mountain mud began to slide down the trails. And nighttime on the mountain is completely dark, with no city lights around. Finding Kelly in these conditions would be impossible. They decided that they would pick up the trail again in the morning, beginning their search at this spot.

With each passing day, Kelly's mother had become more and more frustrated that her little girl had not been found. She demanded to be let out on the mountain to help with the search. But with Blair out there, still running around armed and considered very dangerous, for her own safety they just couldn't let her. Despite these warnings, however, she and two of Kelly's uncles threw caution to the wind and decided to take their chances and go out to look for Kelly on their own.

Before Matt and Jeff could reach the search area the next day, a call came in from the water company, stating that two of their workers had seen a man resembling Blair in the woods that morning up on another part of the mountain. They'd tried to lure him into their truck with offers of food, but he'd ended up running off again. The detectives headed to the spot where Blair had been spotted, but he was nowhere to be found.

On their way back from the site they received another call—the answer to a prayer that they'd thought might never come: Kelly Sellers's body had been found. With thousands of acres of grueling terrain to search, Kelly's family had gone straight to where her body was buried, as if led there by the hand of God. It was on the same trail where Matt and Jeff had stopped the

The fallen tree under which Kelly Sellers's body was found.
PHOTO BY SERGEANT DAVID ROBERTSON, COURTESY OF
SEVIER COUNTY SHERIFF'S OFFICE, TENNESSEE

night before, right where they had seen the hesitation tracks by the fallen tree. A total of four days had elapsed since Kelly had last been seen alive.

What the family had spotted on the ground in daylight, just under where the roots of the overturned tree poked out, was freshly disturbed ground, and a small piece of blue tarp sticking out from the dirt. When they saw this disturbance at the base of the fallen tree, they ran to it and pulled back the exposed corner of the tarp. To their horror, an all-too-familiar cat's-eye tattoo, just above the small of Kelly's back, was revealed. Kelly's mother immediately broke down and desperately wanted to claw her daughter from the grave. But the uncles, thinking on their feet, knew not to let her mess with the body until the police arrived, for fear of disturbing the crime scene.

When Jeff and Matt arrived at the base of that now infamous fallen tree, they knew that a new problem had arisen—the family. The mother was not going to leave her little girl's side, and she made damn sure that Matt and Jeff knew it. Frankly, they didn't blame her. Nobody would. But they had a crime scene to work; a nut with a gun was still running around on the mountain; and no one, particularly someone who had given life to this girl, should have to see what would be coming next. The uncles knew that as well. But Kelly's mother plopped herself down on a stump and said that she refused to move until she saw them pull her daughter out of the ground. Luckily, a compromise was reached: if the uncles were allowed to stay with the detectives, the mother would wait at home. This was agreed on, and Kelly's uncles remained nearby, leaving the experts to the most unenviable of tasks.

The first thing Matt and Jeff did at the scene was call for their crime scene truck. When they went to make the call, though, no one was left at the office to bring up the truck except the sheriff himself. However, Sheriff Bruce Montgomery, a tough old veteran of many different walks of law enforcement life, brought the truck to the mountain without hesitation and left in a squad car, never once trying to get involved with the case. Sheriff Montgomery hires good people, trains them well, and lets them do their jobs. Unfortunately, the crime scene truck couldn't make it all the way up the dirt trails to the scene, so eventually an army truck had to be brought in to relay supplies to the top of the trail. The supplies were then carried by hand from the trail down to the burial site.

By this time, the media had heard the news of the body being found from the police scanners and had begun doing what they do best—show up on site and annoy the hell out of the police. Kelly's mother had already seized the opportunity to use the media the day before, to vent the frustration she felt that the sheriff's department wasn't doing enough to find her daughter. However, Kelly's body was found before the piece had aired, taking the wind out of the local reporter's sails. To deal with the media onslaught, the sheriff's department sent one of the other investigators (the one who drew the shortest straw, no doubt) down to the bottom of the mountain to keep watch and say nothing—especially because Blair was still on the loose.

Detective Mark Turner, who was still scouring the hills looking for Blair, was called back to the burial scene to help with the recovery. (Detective Stephanie McClure would miss all of the action, basking in the sun on a vacation she had planned months before this case occurred.) Detectives Matt Cubberley and Jeff McCarter worked lead on the burial recovery scene. Matt and Jeff had never worked one of these scenes, but they had the requisite experience, having been trained to unearth bodies at the outdoor anthropological research facility known as the Body Farm. For more than thirty years, this outdoor forensic laboratory has been devoted to the study of human decomposition. Over time, as the popularity of forensic science skyrocketed, the facility evolved and added human remains recovery to its repertoire. Today it is still the only place in the world where crime scene investigators can practice the proper way to identify a clandestine grave and exhume a human body. So the Sevier County CSIs were up to the challenge that this crime scene brought. Mark's job would be to assist them; at the time of this case, he had yet to attend forensic school, though ironically, he began his training just two weeks later.

. . .

"We decided we'd do it just like an archaeological dig, just like we were taught," Jeff began, as we examined the trowel marks that were still visible, left on the walls of the clandestine grave they had excavated exactly one year earlier. But they didn't start working the scene by exhuming the grave, as many people might think. Most investigators desperately want to begin with the body, unearthing it from the ground as soon as possible. That's a natural instinct, but it's not the proper way to work a burial scene. The first thing they did was to begin their search far from Kelly's grave. They'd learned that patience pays off, and so they started their work away from the body, working slowly toward where she lay. This was the first buried murder victim that Sevier County had ever had, at least as long as anyone could remember, but the detectives knew exactly what to do from the moment they found the body. If it hadn't been for the training they had received, they might never have known how to proceed. Too bad for the killer that they were some of the best students we had ever had graduate from the crime scene school.

. . .

The group diligently worked toward Kelly's body, marking evidence along the way, mixing dental stone for casting tire tracks, and photographically documenting every inch of the crime scene. They searched with such painstaking detail that they even discovered drops of blood on leaves on the ground, as well as a blood smear on a rock that was lying near the overturned tree. It took more than six hours to mark and collect all of the evidence before they even reached the spot where Kelly lay in a shallow grave. The sun had begun to set once again and darkness was creeping in fast by that time, and they had not even touched Kelly's body yet—they knew it was going to be a long night. Generators and lights were brought in so that they could continue to work the scene meticulously, photographing, marking, measuring, scraping, sifting, digging, and collecting, one step at a time. Even Kelly's uncles commented on how impressed they were with the crime scene team's diligence.

Finally, at long last, they reached the buried body wrapped in the tarp. As they excavated the grave, the CSIs tried as best as they could to keep her wrapped in the tarp in order to preserve any evidence that might still be in or on it. They even tried to keep the dirt that was on top of the tarp from moving.

Several things were readily visible once they reached the body and removed it from the grave. Kelly was completely

Sevier County CSIs recovering the body of Kelly Sellers.
PHOTO BY SERGEANT DAVID ROBERTSON, COURTESY OF
SEVIER COUNTY SHERIFF'S OFFICE, TENNESSEE

nude, bound with duct tape at her wrists and ankles. She had a few strands of hair clutched in one of her hands. The folds of the tarp matched the lividity on Kelly's body precisely. Lividity, blood settling in the lower areas of a deceased body, sets in within thirty to forty minutes after death. Because the folds of the tarp interrupted the places where the lividity had settled, it signified to the investigators that she'd been wrapped in the tarp either before she died or within an hour after her death. She also had a large, trailing blood clot that had come from her anus. For blood clots to form and be expelled, an individual must be alive, even only just minimally (as when the heart still beats for several minutes after a fatal trauma has occurred). Both of these observations indicated that she had more than likely been buried alive or at the very least, not long after her death. Once the detectives completed working their scene, they placed Kelly's body in a body bag and, at the request of her uncles, allowed them to assist in transporting her off the mountain.

The postmortem examination conducted by the local medical examiner concluded that Kelly had been struck with a baseball bat—an odd finding for an ME, to narrow it down so specifically. Medical examiners are trained to generalize and not specify, especially without photographic certainty as proof of what they are concluding. Most use phrases such as "blunt force trauma" to describe an injury indicating that something robust, such as a bat, was used. Therefore, the ME's conclusion just did not sit well with Detective Matt Cubberley, particularly because no murder weapon had yet been discovered. Armed with this information, he decided to call in another expert, Dr. James Downs, medical examiner with the Georgia Bureau of Investigation, whom he had met through the forensic school. Dr. Downs was eager to lend his expertise and asked to see the autopsy photos. On reviewing the photographs, Dr. Downs concluded that it was definitely blunt force trauma, but in his opinion the wounds appeared to have been created by something with a broader surface area than a baseball bat—if he had to guess, something more akin to a brick or a large rock. (They tested the rock found lying near the grave with a blood smear on it, but it did not match the wounds on Kelly's body, so it was determined not to be the murder weapon.)

Matt also asked about the lividity that he had observed, and Dr. Downs agreed with what they had surmised all along—that there was a possibility of Kelly's having been buried alive. He went on to state that in his medical opinion, however, between the amount of blood she had lost and the brutal trauma to her skull, she could not have lived with the injuries she had sustained. The rest of the examination determined that Kelly had also been violently raped vaginally, as well as anally, before her death.

Right after the body had been removed from the grave site, a call came in that Blair had been sighted on the backside of English Mountain, in Cocke County, Tennessee. Detective Derrick Woods, another graduate of the forensic academy, received the call and went to investigate, along with a couple of good ol' bloodhounds. Detectives Mark Turner and Jeff McCarter also received the call and rushed to the scene. The search team met up at the little mom-and-pop market to get ready to go out into the woods to conduct the manhunt. While they were all standing around, Jeff heard someone stirring in the woods. "Shhh, quiet," he whispered to the group. It was none other than John Wayne Blair, the man who had eluded them for several days. Blair yelled out to the investigators, telling them he would come out if they would just keep the dogs away from him. It turned out that Blair was terrified of dogs. So they restrained the barking hounds, and a very haggard, very weary Blair exited the woods with his hands above his head. They immediately grabbed and cuffed him, and within seconds he began acting bizarrely, pecking around like a bird, talking crazy, possibly attempting to lay the groundwork for an insanity defense. Blair was arrested, read his rights, and transported to the Sevier County Sheriff's Office, where they warmed him up and gave him something to eat.

When Blair finished eating his food, the investigators interrogated him. He again started with the crazy act, sitting in the corner, looking wild-eyed all around the room, talking to himself. They continued to question him about Kelly Sellers. Blair

Sevier County's Detective Mark Turner and Cocke County's Detective Derrick Woods escort John Wayne Blair from the woods upon capture.

never asked for an attorney, but he never admitted to killing Kelly either. He repeated the story he'd told Sergeant Hodges days earlier, that he'd been with her that Friday night and then had taken her home. But, as would become a theme, Blair accused Tommy Humphries of being the culprit, claiming that *he* was the one who had killed Kelly.

Indeed, Tommy did seem to know a lot of details about Kelly's disappearance, not to mention where she had been buried. Later, after Blair's arrest and subsequent incarceration, a jailhouse snitch informed the CSIs that Blair had told him that Humphries had killed Kelly, going into great detail, even saying that she had miraculously sat up in the back of Humphries's truck as he drove her body up the mountain to bury her. Tommy Humphries, however, to the chagrin of the defense, passed a lie detector test with flying colors, scoring as high as one possibly can on the truth scale when questions about Kelly's death were asked. But killers typically talk about their deeds—they cannot help it—and Blair's statements to the snitch seemed very truthful. He probably portrayed how the events of Kelly's death unfolded accurately, with one major omission: He left out the part where he was the culprit, not Tommy.

At one point during Blair's interrogation, Matt and Jeff went back into a "good cop/bad cop" routine, showing Blair a picture of Kelly as she had been alive. The picture that they used was her driver's license photo. It had been inexplicably mailed to them, from an anonymous source, while they were hunting for Blair. They asked him if that was Kelly in the picture, and he answered, "Yes, she's my friend." Then they showed a picture of her lying dead and bloody in the tarp, and asked him why he had done that to her. He tore up the second picture, threw it down on the floor, and called them all crazy. That's when he finally decided to ask for an attorney. He paused just enough from his insanity act to realize that he was in trouble.

Once Blair was behind bars, the CSIs got to work on their case for court, submitting the evidence that they had collected to the lab for analysis. The investigators wanted to match the hairs found in Kelly's hand to John Blair. Unfortunately, there were no roots attached to the shafts of hair she had pulled out. Therefore, the only test the lab could run was a mitochondrial DNA profile and not a full comparison. Although a full DNA profile could have narrowed the sample down to one particular person, the mitochondrial profile can narrow the population down significantly only to a familial DNA type on a mother's side of the family. The results that came back from the lab could not say that the hairs in Kelly's hand were specifically John Blair's, but they did show that the hairs definitely came from someone in John's immediate family (his mother or brother), which certainly helped whittle down the field of suspects.

Laboratory analysis also confirmed that all of the blood found at Blair's house—the blood on the bucket, the door, the carpet, and the back of the truck bed—was indeed Kelly Sellers's blood. The investigators also matched the tire tracks found at the burial scene to the tires on Blair's truck, but they could only say it was the same tread and not the exact same tire. The tires were too new to have any distinguishing characteristics of wear. With the totality of the physical evidence; the suspect's having fled, armed, into the mountains; and the previous similar case Blair had been convicted of in Florida, all signs seemed to point to John Wayne Blair as Kelly Sellers's killer. But it would ultimately be up to a jury to decide.

The prosecution was convinced that the physical evidence, particularly the mitochondrial DNA evidence, would stand on its own in court, proving beyond a reasonable doubt to the jury that John Blair had killed Kelly Sellers. The defense's main argument for Blair's innocence was that while incarcerated, John had told a fellow inmate and a jailer what he claimed was the *real* story of what happened on the night Kelly was murdered. Blair's story, of course, continued to be that Tommy Humphries was responsible for Kelly's death, though he now offered many more details, including that he and Humphries had both been high on hallucinogens, and that they had both had sex with Kelly. But he also continued to claim no involvement with her death. And although evidence showed that Kelly had been sexually assaulted, no bodily fluids or fingerprints were found on her body to single out either man. The only evidence implicating another person was the hairs she had clenched in her hand.

The prosecution used the FBI's mitochondrial laboratory to have the hair evidence analyzed and presented in court. The analysis stretched the protocol of mitochondrial analysis beyond the bounds of the traditional testing. It would be not only the first time that mitochondrial evidence was ever admitted in a Sevier County courtroom, but the first time that this advanced type of analysis had ever been admitted as evidence in any courtroom anywhere.

The totality of the evidence against Blair convinced the twelve-person jury that he was guilty of first-degree murder for the rape, torture, and death of Kelly Sellers. They deliberated for only four hours. If not for the painstaking care the crime scene investigators had taken looking for the evidence at the scene, the case might not have turned out the same. Circumstantial evidence can take a case only so far, and eyewitness testimony would have ended with two English Mountaineers pointing fingers at one another. In the age of the CSI Effect, jurors have come to expect hard evidence and scientific analysis to connect a suspect to a crime scene. The Sevier County investigators gave the jury just that.

After John Blair's conviction, the jury still had to decide on what sentence he would serve for his horrific crime. Throughout the trial, doctors informed the jury about Blair's mental condition, placing his IQ at or below seventy—the score of someone considered to have mild retardation. His mother also testified in court about the abuse he had endured when he was a child. Included in her testimony were tales of beatings by his father, a Ku Klux Klan member who forbade John to attend church or school. John Wayne Blair had only a third-grade education. The jury was also informed of Blair's previous conviction in Florida for sexual battery and the fact that he was a regis-tered sex offender. The sentencing testimony ended with Blair's mother in tears, begging the jury to spare her son's life.

After just a short time, the jury brought back a sentence of life without the possibility of parole, sparing Blair's life. In a very unusual act, Blair addressed the jury, thanking them for not giving him the death penalty and further saying "I know I'm not going to hell for killing anybody; I didn't." On March 17, 2007, Blair was moved from the Sevier County Jail to the Brushy Mountain Correctional Complex—the same facility where the infamous James Earl Ray, assassin of Dr. Martin Luther King, Jr., remained until his death. Within four days of being admitted to his new residence, he was assaulted, sup-posedly for a comment he made about another inmate's girl-friend—proof yet again that there is at least some honor among thieves.

· · ·

Today, a small wooden cross marks the place where Kelly Sell-ers's body was found. It's a simple monument, two sticks tied together with a small piece of brown twine, in remembrance of where Kelly was removed from her earthen tomb. A sun-faded soft drink can marks the top of the trailhead leading down to the rudimentary memorial. When we visited the site, with the sun permeating magnificently through the trees, it marked the one-year anniversary of Kelly Sellers's murder. The experience was sobering, to say the least.

Seeing that setting on English Mountain up close was a truly remarkable experience. And even though it had been a year since they had dug up Kelly Sellers, you could still smell a hint of death in the air. That smell never, ever completely dissipates. A distinctly somber mood hung over us as we walked down to the roots of that overturned tree. There was an unplanned and unrehearsed moment when no one spoke and no one moved. Eventually we began speaking again, and we talked at length about the case, all of us wondering aloud how Blair must have felt as he drove his truck over the ragged terrain exactly 2.1 miles from his house, nostrils still filled with the stench of bleach and—given his story—at one point probably seeing Kelly sit up in the back of his truck bed in his rearview mirror. How she must have felt as he dragged her probably live and very battered body over that uprooted tree as she bled out into the tarp, spending her last few minutes on earth buried alive. And how did he do it? There were no drag marks to be found. Did he throw Kelly over his shoulder and carry her down there by himself? John Wayne Blair is not a big man. Did he have help burying her? We may never fully know. Ninety-nine times out of a hundred, a killer will confess to everything but the "how." So far, Blair has admitted to nothing. Nevertheless, the conversation gave us all a chill as we considered just how cruel people can really be.

When we started back up the hill to leave, the CSIs began reminiscing about their time at the academy and telling tall tales exaggerated by time. They told us they wouldn't trade their experiences for anything. These people truly epitomize what it means to be a "good ol' boy"—a gender-neutral term, of course. It means that you work hard, you play hard, and you help others when you can. Yes, these guys can be rambunctious, but they are some of our closest friends and greatest allies. It doesn't matter what we ask for; anything we ask, they will do it for us. And even though it's been a few years since Sevier County had a CSI come through the program, a mysterious mason jar filled to the brim with a clear liquid always seems to make it to an academy class—even if for medicinal purposes only.

2

The Crying Game

BOONE COUNTY SHERIFF'S OFFICE, KENTUCKY

BOONE COUNTY

KENTUCKY

Boone County is the north-ernmost county in the state of Kentucky, and it sits right on the bank of the Ohio River. Founded in 1798, it is currently one of the fastest growing counties in the country. Boone County was named after Daniel Boone, a frontiersman from Tennessee. The county seat is Burlington. Though Boone County has the feel of a small town, it can have the crime of a large metropolitan area because Cincinnati is directly across the river. In fact, the Cincinnati/Northern Kentucky International Airport sits right in the heart of Boone. The Boone County Sheriff's Office is the second-largest agency in the state and one of only two sheriff's offices in Kentucky accredited by the KACP (Kentucky Association of Chiefs of Police). The average time it takes Boone County detectives to make an arrest is less than sixteen hours. The crime scene investigation team consists of one forensic technician, one detective, and two patrol officers.

I want the truth!" a crazed Tom Cruise yelled at Jack Nicholson in the classic military courtroom drama *A Few Good Men*. The movie is filled with rich theatricality and poignant drama, not unlike many courtrooms across the country. Somewhere, every day, a prosecutor is working on a case, studying the facts, trying to put a criminal behind bars. And at the same time, a defense attorney somewhere is trying to poke holes through an argument for putting a criminal behind bars. The American judicial concept of "innocent until proven guilty" is geared almost entirely to the rights of defendants—their state of mind and their actions. Unfortunately, the victim often gets lost in the mix, buried under six feet of dirt and forty feet of briefs. But there are pockets all across the country where justice still means punishing people for the bad things they have done. We were fortunate enough to find one of those pockets in Boone County, Kentucky.

"There's a lot of stuff we know should be here but it's missing—not just a murder weapon." This is how prosecutor Linda Tally Smith of Boone County, Kentucky, began her closing argument in the Beckham hotel murder case. It is not unusual for Linda to turn her back to the judge and begin a vigorous, tear-filled rant not only about why the defendant should be brought to justice but also about why the family of the victim should be brought peace. She sometimes falls to her knees, like a Church of God parishioner overcome with the Holy Spirit about to speak in tongues. An old southern Kentucky gentleman prosecutor once told her to do that when she could, almost certainly guaranteeing a victory when performed just right. Not every judge puts up with the teary closing, though the Supreme Court has determined that lawyers are human (a sometimes disputable point) and are therefore allowed to show emotion in the courtroom. But—to use a local southern expression—that dog sometimes doesn't hunt in Kentucky, and Linda's been warned by more than one judge about crying in the courtroom (she refers to this as the perils of being a "chick prosecutor"). She just turns her back to the judge, flips a mental bird and, though *verklempt*, continues pressing on with her argument just waiting for the prime opportunity to fall to her knees.

We met prosecutor Linda Tally Smith on the second floor of the Huntington Bank building in Boone County, Kentucky. It's an odd place for an office that houses the most powerful woman in the entire county. At the time of her election to office in 2000, she was the youngest and only female prosecutor in the

Commonwealth of Kentucky. The county is hardly known for its liberalism—in fact, Boone County has the largest Republican population in the state. Smith's own Republicanism is illustrated by several prominently displayed autographed pictures of "W" holding each of her three kids. Yet the Dixie Chicks CD—the all-girl band from Texas that famously clashed with the Bush administration—on Smith's desk also speaks to a certain amount of youthful liberalism, and that aura certainly permeates her entire office. Exuberance and playful banter reign supreme here and signify in many regards the "new way" of doing business in this area; a law enforcement renaissance, so to speak.

Linda had always wanted to be a prosecutor, even as a child. "I remember the big ones," she says, while checking the continuous stream of e-mails that ding on her computer, referring to the many cases she can recall having followed during her Kentucky childhood. One in particular, the Eugene Gall murder case, happened in 1979 when Linda was nine years old. Gall kidnapped twelve-year-old Lisa Jansen as she walked to school, then raped and shot her. That violent crime had an incredible impact on Linda and has stayed with her throughout her life. A Boone County jury found Gall guilty, though he was mentally impaired, and sentenced him to die—the first person sentenced to death after the reinstatement of the death penalty in Kentucky.

The case floundered for more than twenty years on appeals, Gall never paying his penalty, until the case finally wove its way through the court system in 2001. Ultimately, the original decision was overturned because of the unconstitutionality of not considering Gall to be insane. "It's a true American tragedy," Linda told reporters after the decision came down. A case like that one is what makes Linda who she is. But even in her wildest dreams, she never thought she would be the commonwealth's attorney by the young age of thirty. But sometimes destiny cannot be avoided, and things work out for a reason. Married with three kids, Smith wears her prosecutorial blue blazer in court with a pink blouse to "show her feminine side," confident and considered by many to be the most intimidating person they have ever met. "It's amazing to me that people think that," Linda tells us as we joke about a questionable e-mail she forwarded to her male colleagues in the office. To us, she's just like we are—hardworking but laid back, loves to laugh. Just don't end up on the wrong side of the fence in her county. As the Boone County CSIs, who are also graduates of our program, say, "She is a bulldog, and she bites."

In times past, before Linda was elected to office, the defense lawyers in the area ruled the roost. According to Linda, the term *prosecutor* had become largely trivialized, and defense attorneys took control, informing the prosecution what they would take as a plea deal, instead of the prosecutors making the offer themselves. Often, that's how the cases would be adjudicated; unfortunately, this is still a common practice. The reasons are many, but it can frequently be attributed to burnout, either from the police making good cases that lazy prosecutors

Boone County Sheriff's Department, Kentucky, personnel: Tim Carnahan and Brian Cochran, along with Boone County prosecutor Linda Tally Smith.
HALLCOX & WELCH, LLC

won't prosecute or from bad cases that the prosecution can't do anything with. Eventually, one or both give up and take an easy deal. "I don't think you guys realize the effect the academy has had on building better cases," Linda goes on to explain. "In the past, the focus was always on making arrests and hoping we got more from there. To be truthful, some of the best evidence we got in murder cases was after a defendant was arrested and he was sitting in jail blabbering to other inmates—jailhouse snitches were our best witnesses in those cases. But that's all changed."

In 2002 Sheriff Michael Helmig of the Boone County Sheriff's Department, in Kentucky, decided that his department would have the best crime scene unit in the country—period. In order to do that, he first wanted all of his crime scene investigators to get the best training available, and so he sent them to the National Forensic Academy. Once they graduated from the academy, he dedicated them to working crime scenes exclusively. Today three graduates of the program work in his department, two specifically dedicated to the unit—Detectives Tim Carnahan and Brian Cochran. And Linda works very closely with them, not only to understand the cases they work but to better understand what they do to gather the evidence—and how they do it. That way, she can talk intelligently in court about the case. Many prosecutors across the country view their offices as private islands, completely separate from that of law enforcement. "I've never believed that, because I believe it is my job to work closely with them to build better cases," Linda says, almost frustrated with her counterparts. And it really is the evidence that makes or breaks a case.

"I tried a homicide case one time where I only had Polaroids of the crime scene and that was it," Linda said to us, with a smirk. "Not to mention that when I needed copies of the photographs for the defense for discovery, they took Polaroids of the Polaroids." (Note: This was not the year 1960, but the year 2000!) "The resources the training provided encouraged them to try things out, like [using] plenty of film, et cetera." Now, it's almost the opposite problem in Boone County—too many pictures. But you can never have too many pictures of a crime scene, and you can never collect too much relevant evidence. In fact, since the graduates have begun practicing their craft in Boone County, murders have been solved at an unbelievable clip. Within forty-eight hours of a crime, the Boone County investigators often have a case made and a suspect behind bars. In the Boone County Sheriff's Office, 68 percent of all violent crimes were cleared by the criminal investigation division. According to the department's annual report, there has not been one unsolved homicide since 2001. Compared to the national average for clearing homicides—40 percent—that's incredible. And murders don't happen very often anymore in Boone County. The word is out among criminals: stay out of Boone County. John T. Snow sure wished *he* had.

• • •

"I knew I was in trouble when I saw the Boone County sign," a heavily medicated John T. Snow slobbered from the Kentucky State Penitentiary, the prison where he is currently serving a life sentence for brutally killing Patricia Volpenhein. "I got friends in Kenton County [a county adjacent to Boone] who got ten years for doing something like what I did, but you guys hung me out to dry here." Snow had been out of prison for only six months when he found himself back in jail again, this time for life. He was well aware of the potential price he'd pay by dumping Volpenhein's body into Boone County. But with darkness looming and a taillight out, not to mention a dead body in the bed of his truck, he got nervous. He stopped just short of the county sign, in a field adjacent to a dump, and dragged her lifeless body onto the ground into what he thought was Kenton County. Unfortunately for him, he dragged her a little too far.

Part of Linda's plea agreement with the defense not to seek the death penalty in Snow's case included allowing the Boone County CSIs to interview Snow on tape to discover what really happened on that terrible Saturday. Killers rarely if ever tell exactly how they did it—but Snow was proud of what he did and how he tried to cover it up.

"Why did you move her body?" Detective Tim Carnahan asked Snow during the interview. John Snow had originally shot, stabbed, and killed Patricia Volpenhein in a different field, then transported her body to the one where she was found. "Because I knew those shell casings would get me caught; you guys could get my prints." Snow had moved Volpenhein's body because he knew that his fingerprints could be lifted from the spent shell casings. Like many prisoners who have nothing better to do while in prison, Snow had also watched too many crime shows on TV.

"I should have used a revolver," a visibly frustrated John Snow continued to tell investigators. Shell casings aren't ejected from a revolver. They stay in the chamber, unlike a pistol, which can eject the casings up to several feet away. Snow would never have moved the body if he hadn't been concerned about the cops finding his prints on the casings, something he'd seen on a television show. But Snow's paranoia was what eventually did him in. According to investigators, it might have been weeks, even months, later by the time the body would have been discovered in its original location. By then, the case would have been cold, and Patricia Volpenhein's killer might never have been found.

Snow and Volpenhein's relationship had been borne out of necessity—she needed heroin, which Snow willingly paid for; he needed sex, which she gave in exchange for the drugs. So they worked out a barter. But it's hard to have a monogamous relationship when you are an addict in constant need of that next high. Unfortunately, John Snow was a very disturbed and jealous person, and when Patricia failed to call him back one day, he decided then and there that he would kill her.

The next day, Volpenhein made the call that she had promised the day before, wanting what she always wanted—more heroin. And Snow obliged, driving her over into Cincinnati, a growing hotbed for heroin ever since the feds had tightened the drug laws for possession of crack. Once she got her fix, they headed to a field for what Volpenhein thought would be her sexual payment for the heroin. Little did she know that it was a place Snow had considered, from the moment he'd seen it years earlier, "a good place to whack somebody." They drove up to the secluded spot and parked the truck. At some point when the two of them had left the vehicle, he casually shot her in the head, and when she went down—"flipping," as he put it—he shot her again in the left temple. "She kept snoring," Snow told the detectives, agitated. Her "snoring" was actually her agonized breathing. She was still clinging to life, despite being fatally wounded by two bullets to the brain. It was clear from watching the interview that the "snoring" had driven Snow crazy; he rocked back and forth as he talked about it. He'd then pulled a cheap knife from his pocket and tried to slice her throat lengthwise like cutting an Easter ham, but the knife was too dull to penetrate the skin deeply enough to finish the job. Instead, he turned to brutally stabbing her several times in the throat. Yet she continued to breathe and "snore."

Feeling that he'd wasted too much time on killing Volpenhein, Snow crawled on the ground, looking for those damn shell casings that he would never find. Panicked, he decided that he couldn't take the chance of those shell casings being found with his fingerprints all over them, so he had to get her body out of that field. His mind raced. In a manic frenzy, he went on a shopping spree, buying plastic tarps, clothes, gloves—all in preparation for disposing of Volpenhein's body. Little did he realize that his actions created more evidence, tying the murder to him.

After purchasing the items he thought he would need, Snow waited for darkness to fall before he went back to the field to retrieve Volpenhein's body. When he arrived, Volpenhein had finally ceased breathing, and he began to carry out his ill-fated plan. He wrapped her in both of the tarps and struggled to get her into the bed of his truck. Once that was complete, he headed down River Road to the mighty Ohio. "I wanted to throw her in the river," Snow told the detectives. The Ohio River has long been a repository for many a perp's victims, harking back to the days when the mob influenced the area. But "I couldn't find a spot on River Road," Snow lamented. Fishermen dotted the banks at various intervals along the river, so he couldn't find a safe spot to stop his truck and dump the body. Frustrated, Snow gave up on his original plan and kept driving in the darkness. And then another fear overwhelmed him. He remembered he had a taillight out. He began to panic even more as he rounded the bend on River Road, which connects Kenton County to Boone County. When his headlights hit the "Entering Boone County" sign, his heart sank. He knew he was in trouble. So he pulled over immediately, swerving to the left into an open field. He jumped out of his truck, ripped down his tailgate, and pulled Volpenhein's body onto the ground. Having been so afraid of leaving his fingerprints on the shell casings, he knew to wear gloves when he moved her body. He'd worn them when he removed the tarps from the packaging. He'd worn them when he rolled her lifeless body onto the first tarp and had kept them on as he wrapped her tightly into the second one. He'd worn them when he struggled to get her body into the back of his pickup truck. He'd even worn them as he drove alongside the Ohio River looking for the perfect dump site. But with too many scenarios for his borderline IQ to process, he forgot to wear them as he dumped her to the earth and into Boone County.

On the Sunday afternoon that followed, after a horrible night's sleep, Snow's paranoia returned and began to get the best of him. It occurred to him that he might not have been wearing his gloves when he dumped Volpenhein's body, and he decided to go back to the field to retrieve the tarps. But when he arrived, "I saw police everywhere," Snow said, never once showing any remorse for anything except not being able to find those shell casings and stupidly forgetting to wear his gloves. Again he panicked, removing his tailgate and bed liner with a pair of pliers, tossing them into a Dumpster, and fleeing to his brother's house in Tennessee (where he was not welcomed with open arms). He ultimately returned to Kentucky and nervously awaited his fate, while Boone County detectives began working the case.

· · ·

"The academy taught us, if nothing else, to think outside the box," Detective Brian Cochran told us as the three of us, along with Detective Tim Carnahan, took mountain curves at high speeds, en route to one of the hidden treasures of Boone County—a place called Rabbit Hash. Rabbit Hash is an odd little place with a population bordering on one or two, with a newly elected Labrador retriever as the town's mayor. At least it was a close race. The pig that ran against the retriever was a formidable candidate, but his platform didn't resonate quite as well with the populace as the retriever's. Good ol' Kentucky.

Detective Tim Carnahan was the second person from Boone County to go through the academy's program. Before he came through the program in 2003, Tim was admittedly retirement bound, burned out, tired of working scenes just to see

The Rabbit Hash General Store in Boone County, Kentucky.
HALLCOX & WELCH, LLC

the cases get pleaded out. Our program infused new life into him and his work, which Linda Tally Smith and everyone else could see. After reaching Rabbit Hash, we stood looking out on the banks of the Ohio River, drinking peach soda pops and sarsaparillas, talking about the academy, the sheriff's department, and the John T. Snow murder case. "We've got great support from our sheriff," Detective Carnahan said. They really do have a lot of support from the whole county. The synergy in all of Boone County is incredible. A brand-new sheriff's office with state-of-the-art facilities allows the CSIs to hone their craft when crime happens to take a night off. They are the best at taking what they have learned and making it better. That is particularly true of Detective Brian Cochran, whom Smith affectionately calls "Beaker" or "Bill Nye the Science Guy." We like to call him "CSI MacGyver." He can make a forensic tool out of just about anything. Cochran is part of the new, younger generation of CSIs, who really push the limits of the science behind crime scene investigation. If he needs a piece of equipment, he simply builds it rather than paying hundreds of dollars from a forensic supply store. We visited the lab with Brian and Tim and saw many items that were as well made as, probably better than, some of the fancy things for sale. Cochran is fortunate that his department lets him be creative and play with new ideas and new techniques. And it's paid off for them.

"Most of what we do isn't written down somewhere," Detective Carnahan went on to explain. "Sometimes the thing you do on a crime scene is the first time it's been done." That's very true. Forensic science is much like law or medicine—it is a practicing art. Not only does the science change each year, but the environment CSIs deal with differs with every call. Each situation they face presents new and unique challenges. "How do you string a bloodstain in a trailer hallway, with that really nasty and greasy shag carpet that nothing will stick to?" Detective Carnahan said, referencing a recent case. "You simply must improvise." And they do—in that case, by fashioning fishhooks from safety pins (which Detective Carnahan's wife provided by running to the store) and hooking one end into the carpet and the other end to the colored string. In Boone County, working crime scenes can truly be a team effort.

This synergy and broad view of crime scene investigation is really what nailed John Snow to the murder of Patricia Volpenhein. Despite his paranoia, the evidence he left at the scene was limited: the two tarps, a glove, and tread wear from the truck. The glove and tread wear are typical of the kinds of evidence that can be photographed, cast, or collected. But the tarps, two eight-by-ten blue plastic tarps, presented a unique challenge. "Before the academy, I wouldn't have processed the tarps," Detective Carnahan told us as we got back into the vehicle to head back to the sheriff's department. But now, he said, "Instead of looking at things as if we could not process them, we now look at everything as something that *can* be processed; that broad perspective is what your training provided to us."

Television has provided viewers, and therefore potential jurors, with the unrealistic expectation that all CSIs are like the ones found in prime time. Unfortunately, that could not be any further from the truth. We have held classes on developing latent fingerprints in which thirty-year veterans in the field had no idea that a fingerprint could be lifted off anything other than something smooth, like a piece of glass. Imagine working crime scenes for thirty years without having the background to know how to develop prints off all types of surfaces? How many more crimes could have been solved?

Looking for a fingerprint on two eight-by-ten tarps (front and back) is like looking for a needle in a haystack. But the only way to find that needle *is* to look, and look is what Detective Carnahan did. He decided that in order to process the tarps, he needed to superglue-fume them. Common, everyday superglue, dabbed into a small pan and heated, causes the glue to give off gaseous vapors that stick to the ridges of an oily fingerprint and make it more readily visible. On larger items, a fan is sometimes used to help circulate the vapors throughout the container. In order to superglue-fume something, however, the item must be completely contained so that the entire surface area is exposed. Carnahan studied the situation and jotted down a schematic for a large frame that he wanted the maintenance guys at the sheriff's department to create. The frame would allow the tarp to hang completely inside the container with both sides exposed. The real ingenuity came when, instead of building solid walls, he decided to contain the fumes with plastic wrap—industrial plastic wrap, like the kind used to wrap pallets for shipment on trucks. In essence, Carnahan made a large box using the plastic wrap for the sides. This made it easy to put the tarp and the superglue in the container, along with a fan to help circulate the fumes. It also allowed him to put a test print, his own, on the inside of the plastic to know that the process was working. With his superglue-fuming contraption in place, he simply wrapped the frame tightly and let the tarp fume. This procedure was performed twice, once on each tarp.

"I then simply cut the plastic and removed the tarp," Detective Carnahan told us as we all walked down the corridor in the sheriff's department to where all of the evidence is kept. The two tarps were still evidence at the time, but the case had just gone through all of its appeals, and the defense had failed. Snow's fate was sealed. The sentence would stand for eternity, and the evidence could now be opened. "I then took the tarps and went over them inch by inch with a finger-print loupe looking for ridge detail"—the fine lines of a finger-print—Carnahan explained as he and Cochran located the tarps still sealed in large brown paper evidence bags. Detec-tive Carnahan had gone over the tarps closely, front and back, using a Sharpie to circle areas that had at least *some* ridge detail. Then he hit those areas with a fluorescent dye stain to enhance the prints' visibility so he could use a forensic light source to bring out more detail. And there it was—a nearly complete left thumbprint. "The guys who run AFIS [Auto-mated Fingerprint Identification System—the searchable data-base of fingerprinted criminals] laughed when they heard I was trying to develop a print off a tarp," Carnahan told us as we stood watching him and Cochran lay the tarp out on the floor of the police department garage, rehydrating the print by spray-ing it with the dye stain Ardrox so we could see it better. With the hum of the light source in the background, Carnahan and Cochran jumped around the tarp like elves, looking for just the right angle to view the print in detail. Though time and folding had changed the clarity somewhat, there the print was, right in front of us, about five feet up from a deep maroon-colored stain: the color of dried postmortem blood—Patricia Volpenhein's blood. It was eerie to see the evidence up close and

Brian Cochran and Tim Carnahan examining the tarp for fingerprint evidence.
HALLCOX & WELCH, LLC

personal, and amazing that Carnahan had ever found the print in the first place.

. . .

With the print developed, Carnahan needed a good picture to send to the guys at AFIS for comparison in the nationwide database, in order to see if there was a match. The first picture had a little bit of a wave from the tarp, which made it difficult for the guys to put into AFIS. But the next picture was perfect, and within hours a hit popped up on the screen—John T. Snow.

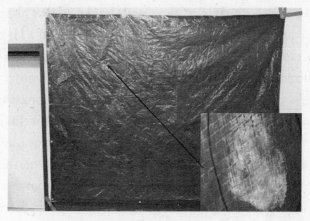

Latent fingerprint that was found on the tarp. The print
matched John Snow's.
PHOTO BY TIM CARNAHAN, OFFICE OF THE COMMONWEALTH'S ATTORNEY,
54TH JUDICIAL CIRCUIT

Forgetting to wear his gloves was Snow's first mistake—
and leaving one behind would be his last. In order for a murder
to be a capital offense in most states, meaning a death penalty case, there needs to be more than just murder for murder's sake. It seems ridiculous, but there must be extenuating
circumstances, such as multiple homicides, extraordinary violence, or rape. Premeditation alone won't necessarily do it (and
in this instance, the knowledge of premeditation only came out
of Snow's interview *after* his plea). This gave Snow's attorneys
some hope that they might be able to mitigate Snow's punish-
ment and avoid the death penalty. But Carnahan wasn't finished with the evidence. Almost as an afterthought, Carnahan
processed the glove that had also been found at the scene. It

was a cotton knit style of glove and, unlike a latex glove, one that would be impossible to retrieve prints from. However, given the ever-increasing sensitivity of DNA testing, Carnahan decided to send the glove to the lab to see if any epithelial cells could be recovered. Knowing it was a long shot, he also sent the rape kit that had been done on Volpenhein, just in case there was anything to compare the evidence to. And there was. John Snow's skin cells were found not only on the interior of the gloves but also on Volpenhein. With that evidence, the case became a capital murder trial because it appeared now that John Snow might have raped Patricia Volpenhein. When confronted with that evidence, Snow went crazy, showing the only emotion he ever displayed over Volpenhein throughout the whole ordeal. It wasn't that he cared that he'd killed her (according to him, she was an old drug whore who deserved it); it was that he didn't want to be "falsely" accused of doing something that he claimed he didn't. He was adamant that he didn't rape Volpenhein and that their sex was consensual. But to a jury, it would appear that rape was at least a possibility, and therefore the case would become capital in nature. Plus other evidence was mounting up against him as well. The tire impressions taken from the field were of an odd pattern, with three of the four tires having the same style tread, but with a different tread on the fourth tire, more of a snow tread. Just like the tires on John Snow's truck. Furthermore, as the detectives in the case continued to work, they discovered video evidence of John Snow buying two blue plastic tarps at an AutoZone store. They also obtained video surveillance footage from the dump site that showed Snow's red truck, missing taillight and all, driving around the facility as it was getting dark, on the night that Volpenhein's body was dumped. All pretty convincing evidence—absolutely none of which would have ever been created if it hadn't been for Snow's paranoia about those shell casings with his fingerprints on them (which, incidentally, have *never* been found). No tarps would have been purchased and no fingerprints would have been left—nothing. Yet everything he did to cover up his guilt simply dug his grave a little deeper. Sometimes the CSI Effect does have its advantages; using what he learned from television actually caused Snow's downfall.

• • •

With our examination of the tarp over, the boys folded it back up and sent it to the incinerator, clearing the way for new and probably bloodier evidence.

The next morning, we were back in that "odd place for a prosecutor to practice law" building, wrapping up the Beckham case that we had begun discussing when we first convened. "Rodney Beckham was a prolific liar," prosecutor Linda Tally Smith said disdainfully of the defendant. Indeed, he was no saint. He already had a long rap sheet, including two felonies, and was a known drug addict and dealer when on July 2, 2004, he was arrested for the attempted murder of twenty-seven-year-old Stacy Beals. The trial lasted seven days. Much evidence was examined and many witnesses were called in, including doctors who discussed in detail the brutality of Stacy's injuries. Linda was kind enough to provide us the entire trial on tape so we could watch it and see for ourselves how it had unfolded. Tim Carnahan's and Brian Cochran's testimonies were brilliant, particularly Brian's testimony regarding the bloodstains. He appeared quite scientific when examined by the defense, dispelling Hollywood myths about how blood travels on impact and how much blood they could expect to see. But overall there was little physical evidence, and they were missing the big kicker—no murder weapon had been found. The trial would all come down to whether the jury believed that the Commonwealth of Kentucky had met its burden of proving beyond a reasonable doubt that Rodney Beckham killed Stacy Beals. Ultimately, it would come down to Linda.

• • •

Rodney and Stacy had been out partying well into the morning of June 27, 2004. Eventually, the two of them left together to score some crack cocaine to smoke at the Econo Lodge in Carrollton, Kentucky. At some point between two and five a.m., Stacy was beaten and left for dead. Stacy, barely clinging to life, wasn't found until a hotel maid discovered her as she attempted to clean the room. She had been beaten so severely that pieces of skull were found scattered throughout the hotel room. Rodney Beckham was nowhere in sight.

Word spread throughout the small Kentucky community that Stacy Beals had been hurt and that she'd last been seen

The bloodstained mattress at the Beckham murder crime scene.
PHOTO BY TIM CARNAHAN, OFFICE OF THE COMMONWEALTH'S ATTORNEY,
54TH JUDICIAL CIRCUIT

with Beckham. One of Stacy's friends, who was related to a police officer, called in the tip, and it wasn't long until the hunt was on for Beckham. Rodney had heard that he was being sought after, and so he hid for a couple of days to "sober up" and to get his story straight. Even so, he eventually told the police several different stories to cover his own ass, weaving a bizarre tapestry of lies and half-truths that even he couldn't keep up with. He told stories about buying crack supplies at a Kroger supermarket, including Bic lighters, a Chore Boy (a copper scouring pad commonly used as a filter in a crack pipe), and rubber gloves—to "throw off" the cashier, he said. He told more stories, of leaving Stacy in the hotel room and going back to find her beaten, and others of how he knelt down to hold her head as she moaned, and how her limp neck allowed her head to roll, striking him on the chin and "spattering" fine drops of blood onto his arms and into his eyelashes. He told more imaginative stories of how he touched nothing except a shiny tire gauge that he saw out of the corner of his eye as he fled the room, which he then threw across the motel parking lot. The police never found many items: Stacy's money, underwear, pants; the hotel's television remote and towels; all of the items Beckham claimed to have purchased at Kroger; and whatever was used to beat Stacy. And Beckham told yet even wilder stories of not knowing how a bloody shirt of his ended up in the trash where he lived, and how somebody else must have put it there. Linda would later tell the jury in her closing arguments that he "wouldn't know the truth if it bit him in the butt."

After police discovered that Rodney Beckham was lying to them, not to mention the bloody T-shirt in the trash behind his place of residence, he was arrested for the attempted murder of Stacy Beals. She managed to survive for weeks on life support. But eighty-three days later doctors removed Stacy from life support, and she slipped away forever. Beckham's defense team tried to argue that he couldn't be charged with murder because "she'd be alive if they had left her on life support." But their argument fell on deaf ears, and the charge was amended to murder.

On the final day of trial, the defense called their last witness to the stand—Rodney Beckham. They examined him slowly, methodically, coddling him through his lies, his specious time-line, while ignoring many of the details that mattered most, like the bloody shirt in the garbage (and the blood spatter in his eyelashes). It was almost embarrassing to watch; there was little for them to defend. While Beckham answered the questions on the stand, Linda furiously took notes at her table, her demeanor growing more and more tense every time he spoke. The anger on her face came to a crescendo when Beckham began his tearful sobbing at the very end of his testimony. "I might be a piece of shit to a lot of people, but I'm not a murderer," he told the court, his final words under direct examination. It was now Linda's turn to cross-examine. Up until this point of the trial, she had been very friendly with the witnesses, but her demeanor changed with Beckham. Where the defense was slow, quiet, and unsure, Linda was not.

"Mr. Beckham, you indicated that Stacy was a friend of yours and that you thought a lot of her," Linda began as Beckham continued to wipe away his tears. "Yes, I did," he said, sniffing. "You know what today is?" Linda asked angrily. "Yes, I do," Beckham responded, with an almost glad tone. "And what is it?" Linda asked again of Beckham. "Today is her birthday," Beckham informed the court. "Today is Stacy's birthday," Linda repeated softly and remorsefully, fighting back tears. "Would you have known that prior to this happening?" Linda asked him, with disdain. "No, I would not," Beckham said, hanging his head down low. Linda proved immediately that Beckham could not tell the truth even on the simplest of things, like being close friends with Stacy. Close friends know each other's birthdays. Beckham's inability to tell the truth was a pattern that continued throughout her examination.

As Linda's cross-examination continued, Beckham's mouth became obviously dry. The nauseating sound of his lips and tongue sticking together was noticeable as he tried to wiggle through Linda's bulletproof examination. Sometimes he would go off on rants, telling stories to the jury that no one had ever even heard before, while Linda allowed him to dig his own grave—although from time to time she would jab Beckham almost sarcastically when what he said contradicted something he had said earlier. At one point the defense asked for a recess, in order to get their client off the stand and hush his mouth. Beckham was a liar, a fact that even he had to admit while on the witness stand, saying once that he "was no angel." Linda concluded her cross-examination by walking the court through what she believed Beckham had done, proving him as the culprit in the murder of Stacy Beals. Linda relied on the facts of the case, and not the ruminations of a known liar, as her guide to proving the commonwealth's case.

The defense and the prosecution were both given an hour for closing statements. The defense's only real argument was to claim that although Beckham was admittedly a liar, he wasn't lying now. Not much of a defense. Linda's closing was powerful, teary, and theatrical. She likened what she and her team had done to working a jigsaw puzzle. They had provided the border and some of the pieces inside of the frame; and just as with a puzzle, you don't have to have every piece in place to know what the picture shows. Linda told the jury that indeed, although she would not be able to provide them with every piece of the puzzle, there was enough. And with that, closing arguments concluded. It was up to the jury to determine whether Beckham was a liar or an angel.

In only an hour and a half, the jury came back to the courtroom to present the judge their decision. Rodney Beckham was found guilty of murder in the first degree. With the verdict rendered, the judge moved to the sentencing phase, whereby the jurors would be allowed to hear Rodney's other transgressions for the first time, including his two previous felony convictions. In less than an hour, the jury found Beckham a persistent felony offender and sentenced him to life in prison. He now sits in the Eastern Kentucky Correctional Complex. He will be eligible for parole on January 11, 2026, when Stacy would have been only forty-eight years old.

. . .

As we began to say our good-byes with Linda and the guys, we realized just how much justice means to the people here in Boone County. Linda certainly knows, and she takes it all to heart. Her life is really one of juxtaposition—Republicans and Dixie Chicks, pink shirts and blue blazers, babies and killers. Yet she juggles it all effortlessly. And she's very successful at her job; no one even ran against her in the last election. But success doesn't come without a price. When your job is to go after the criminal element, and you take that job seriously, it is easy to make enemies. And threats are par for the course. "Are you ever scared?" we asked Linda as we gathered our belongings to end our final day in Boone County. "Yes," she told us, mentioning one particularly nasty thug whose case didn't go quite as planned. "Not all cases turn out that well, no matter how hard you work or how good the evidence is," Linda went on to say. Sometimes, juries simply make poorly informed decisions. "If you see a man on video writing a bad check, you don't need a handwriting expert [to prove it]; or if a detective sees a dealer pulling a rock of crack from his mouth, you don't need to run a DNA test on it," she said feistily, on our way out the door. In the end, all any prosecutor can do is to work hard, understand what it is he or she is presenting, and present everything in the best light to get as solid a conviction as possible. But the reality is this—doing good means pissing some bad people off. Tragically, the threat of retribution is real. And in this line of work, you don't view your life in years but in lengths of sentences.

3

Thunder Snow, Aye

DULUTH POLICE DEPARTMENT, MINNESOTA

DULUTH

MINNESOTA

Duluth, Minnesota—the county seat of St. Louis County—sits on the banks of Lake Superior. Before it was a city, the land of Duluth was inhabited by the Dakota and Ojibwa tribes, who grew wild rice, still a staple in many households throughout Minnesota. Founded in 1679, Duluth was once a thriving industrial town that boasted a steel plant and the leading port in the United States. In the early 1970s, the city had to shift its economic focus from industry to tourism. Today Duluth shares its port with Superior, Wisconsin, which together make Twin Ports, one of the major ports on the Great Lakes system. Duluth is known for its year-round cool temperatures, but especially its lake-effect snow, which comes in handy for the yearly dog-sled marathon every February. The Duluth Police Department is the third largest in the entire state of Minnesota, with 175 employees.

Duluth, Minnesota. The Scandinavian Americans who dominate this semi-arctic climate pronounce it "Doo-looth." Essentially, Duluth has two seasons—winter and July. On the one hand, winters in Duluth can be unbearable. It has been known to get so cold that a man can urinate outside and the stream will freeze before it hits the ground—not to mention, it's hell on the penis. But on the other hand, July can be gorgeous, with people jogging around Lake Superior, enjoying a homemade root beer at Fitger's Brewery or a malt down by the shore, and some folks even daring to surf the near-frigid waters. Just don't stay too long, or you might get snowed in.

On March 1, 2007, the 151st anniversary of the founding of St. Louis County, whose county seat is the City of Duluth, we were far from the balmy days of July. Sitting in the Comfort Suites Hotel, we anxiously awaited our second continental breakfast of the day. Sounds good, right? Except that this second

The outside of Fitger's Brewery.
HALLCOX & WELCH, LLC

continental breakfast was being served at seven thirty p.m., during the worst blizzard in the history of Duluth. Hurricane-force winds, two-plus feet of snow, thunder, lightning—all combined to close nearly everything in the entire city. Fortunately, we were saved from starvation by a few hard-boiled eggs, a waffle each, and some questionable breakfast meats.

We had been summoned to this bounty by the few brave hotel staff who remained stranded with us. And as the smells of maple syrup and thawing meat wafted into the air, we could hear the hotel staff talking among themselves. "Ya, dey say dere's thunder wid da snow," one of the staff explained to the other in a thick Minnesotan accent. "Ah, ya don' say," the other replied, neither remarkably moved by the unbelievable weather unfolding.

That's how it is in Duluth. It's snowy; it's cold; and, maybe because of the weather, people just don't seem to get that excited about anything—it's as if their blood is frozen. Most cope with the harsh climate by spending hours on end in their saunas (pronounced "sa-oo-nas"), in keeping with their Scandinavian heritage, or eating a "hotdish" full of meat, vegetables, and a binding ingredient such as canned soup. A hotdish is essentially a casserole popular in Minnesota. Pop the concoction into the oven and bake for thirty minutes—simple and Scandinavian. We later ate an authentic hotdish in the house of an authentic Scandinavian family. And, although we realize that everyone everywhere has had a hotdish of one kind or another, when a hotdish is served in Minnesota by Scandinavians, it just tastes better.

The climate of Duluth can be inhospitable and is essentially smack-dab in wilderness country. Nearly 80 percent of the land in the county is uninhabited, with forests and lakes making up most of the area. Because of this lack of population and the light pollution found in most big cities, Duluth is able to partake in one of nature's greatest events—the aurora borealis.

However, all of this undisturbed nature has contributed to Duluth's newfound popularity. In 2006, it was voted one of the top fifty places to live in America. Nevertheless, just like everywhere else, Duluth is not without its criminal element. Thieves, killers, and crooks, like most other animals, adapt to their environments, regardless of how cold it gets. Crime doesn't stop on account of the weather, no matter how bad it gets or how unappetizing the continental breakfast becomes. And harsh winter conditions wreak havoc on crime scenes, as well as on crime scene investigators.

Two of the most useful pieces of evidence left at a crime scene are usually footwear impressions left in the ground and fingerprints left on objects. The cold, snowy climate can impact both tremendously. For example, after a snowfall of more than about one-quarter of an inch, it becomes virtually impossible to get a good footwear impression. This is because with each step, the shoe carries more snow to the next impression, making the subtle characteristics of the tread impossible to discern. Furthermore, the deeper the snow gets, the more likely that prints left in the snow will cave in on themselves. Not to mention the fact that, when it's snowing or the wind is high (and it usually is), shoe prints can be covered up by the blowing snow and hidden forever.

A crime scene investigator will also have more trouble finding and developing fingerprints in cold weather. One obvious reason is that everybody wears gloves during the winter, so by default fewer fingerprints will be left at a scene. Couple that with the fact that cold climates are usually drier, and therefore a perp's hands will be less oily or sweaty than usual—and in order to leave good fingerprints, hands need to be moist.

The weather also affects how a crime scene is processed. In subzero temperatures, camera batteries wear out after taking just two or three shots, and the ink in a ballpoint pen will freeze within seconds. Bullets fired into the snow burn right through, making it nearly impossible to locate the evidence. In some cases, the Duluth CSIs had to call in the fire department to hose down an entire hillside, washing away the snow, in an effort to find spent bullets.

And don't forget about the toll the weather can take on an investigator. The blinding snow, the all-night crime scenes in freezing temperatures, and the lessons they have all learned about not using their mouths to hold anything. Many Duluthian CSIs have jumped out of their vehicles on a cold, icy night and put their keys into their mouths in order to free up both hands. Unfortunately, this usually results in a reenactment of the classic scene in *A Christmas Story*, except it's a tongue stuck to a set of keys instead of to a flagpole.

This wild winter weather calls for good planning, regardless of which side of the criminal justice system a person is on. Sometimes it even calls for a little old-fashioned ingenuity. This far north, the ground may be frozen solid until May, and people who die during the winter sometimes lie in state in a mausoleum until the spring thaw, when they can finally be buried in the ground. That certainly makes it difficult to bury someone you've just killed. The frozen tundra forces some killers to pick their season or, at the very least, buy a wood chipper (like the scene in *Fargo*). Or, if they are really clever, they time it just right and catch an ice-fishing hole just ripe for a burial spot.

"For God's sakes," Sergeant Eric Rish had said to us when

BEHIND THE YELLOW TAPE

we arrived on the eve of the worst blizzard anyone could remember, trudging through the remnants of the previous week's snow. He was commenting on our "big coats," similar to the one George sported on an infamous episode of *Seinfeld*. "It's not that bad," he scoffed. We met Rish in 2004 during Session VIII, a winter session at the academy. Winters in Tennessee can occasionally be cold and snowy, such as the blizzard of '93, as the natives refer to it, when Knoxville had its worst snow ever—piling on nearly thirty inches in and around the city, crippling it for weeks. But since that time it has rarely snowed, proving that at least in Al Gore's home state, global warming is for real. At least, that is, until Eric showed up, bringing with him both snow and the very first snow-covered exhumation practical exercise.

We had arrived at Rish's house for dinner that night and what we hoped would be our first encounter with a traditional hotdish. Eric and his wife, Kris, are an interesting pair. They both work in law enforcement, and they both work in investigations. Yet their jobs are completely different. Eric is with the Duluth Police Department who investigates crime and puts criminals in prison. Kris is an investigator with the Minnesota State Department of Corrections who investigates prison crimes committed by the people whom her husband helped put in there. Crime, major crime, doesn't end at the prison gates. It continues within the confines of a prison and continues to affect law-abiding citizens on the outside. It's amazing what some criminals are still able to do, from sending threats to their

The Duluth blizzard, February 2007.
HALLCOX & WELCH, LLC

estranged lovers during their phone call time to full orchestra-
tion of gang activities. Essentially, it's the effed-up circle of
criminal life. Eric investigates criminals and puts them behind
bars, and Kris keeps on investigating them until they are put to
death or released back into society, where Eric begins his work
all over again.

Kris told us about her side of the law enforcement world
over our hotdish and frosted mugs filled with Fitger's Brewery
root beer. We hadn't planned on researching prisons and prisoners, but when the opportunity came to spend the day with
Kris touring prisons, including one of Minnesota's oldest and
meanest institutions, we said what the hell.

The Stillwater prison is located about thirty-five minutes south of Duluth. Its population is roughly three thousand inmates. It smells like a cross between a school cafeteria, a locker room, a morgue, and a rhino's ass. Stillwater is a maximum-security prison, housing the worst of the worst. At various "free" times, murderers, rapists, and even serial killers roam about the facility at will.

Entering any prison is a very disheartening and disturbing experience. Entering a prison like Stillwater is even worse. We had to give our driver's licenses to the guards (so that in case something happened to us while we were on the inside, they could identify us), get our hands stamped as if we were going to a club, and pass through several very thick steel gates before arriving at the main part of the facility. And when the last gate opened up, we entered, for the first time, the place where we help put the bad guys away. It was akin to waking up in hell.

The prison cells flanked both sides of the main portal, five stories tall, stacked on top of one another like cubes. Ten-by-ten single-dwelling cubes—if they were lucky. Those not so lucky had to share their ten-by-ten space with a roommate. We walked slowly down one of the corridors, with the cells to our left and an old brick wall with a bank of pay phones on our right. We were looking at the prisoners as if they were animals in a zoo. And they were looking at us as if we were food. Some were reading, some were watching television, and all of them were staring. Right away, our guide, Tee—one of the investigators at Stillwater—told us not to get too close to the cells, but also not to stand too far away from them either. This was because being either too close or too far out increased the chance of having bodily fluids being hurled at you, similar to Clarice Starling's ejaculate experience in *The Silence of the Lambs*. Except any experience of ours would be real.

At one point we were cornered in the chow line, with about five hundred of the worst of the worst walking by, many of whom were doing life without the possibility of parole. One of the convicts was reportedly the infamous Harvey Carrigan, serial killer extraordinaire, who leered at us all as if we were some sort of human dessert. And then came the catcalls, from which *none* of us were excluded, male or female. A vile, palpable, nauseating sense of wickedness permeated the place, the likes of which neither of us had ever experienced. As evening approached, we were offered the opportunity to have dinner before we left, cooked and served by some of Stillwater's finest, something with Alfredo sauce, no less. We passed on the opportunity.

Prisons are like cities unto themselves. When a prisoner arrives in Stillwater, he is first placed into a multiperson cell. With time and good behavior, he can apply for a job and possibly upgrade his digs, eventually earning a cell to himself. Prisoners apply for jobs, get jobs, get paid, get fired, earn free time, and buy groceries, television sets, coffee pots, candy bars, sodas, and so on. Prisons are essentially mini-metropolises for the seedy underworld. The old adage that crime doesn't pay is false. It pays roughly twenty-five cents per hour to start in

Minnesota. And with cigarettes going for about three dollars apiece and jailhouse tats going for about forty bucks, many hours have to be put in to afford such luxuries. Not that those luxuries are legal. Sometimes, instead of purchasing their brand of vice, they just make it themselves—in the toilet. Homemade alcohol or hooch is easily made from a little water, a little ketchup, and a little bread. Presto, a ketchup wine that Emeril himself wouldn't even taste. Around the Super Bowl, extra guards have to be brought in to simply do bed checks for all of the hooch contraband made for the event. Gotta love football.

The guards at Stillwater do not carry guns. On average, there are seven or eight major incidents a day, including violent fights with some unbelievable homemade weapons. We saw every type of item imaginable sharpened into deadly weaponry—toothbrushes, plastic forks, shower curtain rings. The one amazing thing about prisoners and prison life is the ingenuity that it breeds. If necessity is the mother of invention, then these mothers really have it. With nothing but time to think, these guys can come up with just about anything. For example, an entrepreneur has contracted with Moose Lake Prison, the prison where Kris Rish works, to have the inmates remove all identifying markings from returned merchandise from Wal-Mart, Target, and the like, which arrives by the truckload, which he then sells in town by the pallet. Moose Lake Prison is also known as the tattoo capital of Minnesota, and enterprising inmates who work in this returns department from time to time break open a VCR, a DVD player, or the video controller to a video game system, and in a split second pull out the little motor to make a tattoo gun. It also helps that Moose Lake Prison has one of the best print shops in all of Minnesota, giving the prisoners access to all of the colors of the rainbow. You just have to admire someone who will take the vibrating motor out of a wireless Xbox 360 controller, shove it up his ass, jerry-rig an electrical plug to it, steal a needle and some ink, and start his own tattoo business at forty dollars a pop. Capitalism, even in prison, is alive and well.

A prisoner's thinking time goes to more than just ways to make money or to survive. Many focus their thoughts on how to get out of the place. Prison breaks are a real possibility day in and day out. Movies like *Escape from Alcatraz* and *The Shawshank Redemption* depict incredible escapes that are not much different from some that we heard about while we were in Minnesota. One story we remember in particular was about a prisoner who had been working on his escape for years. He hacksawed through the bars in his cell and stole newspapers that he fashioned into the shape of cell bars and painted silver to look like the real ones. Every night he sneaked out of his paper cell and went on recons to search for the best route to escape, climbing up onto one of the windows and beginning the painstaking task of sawing through more metal bars. With his route established, he made the final decision to leave. He stuffed his bed with blankets and pillows to make it look like he was still asleep—pretty basic, something that many teenagers have done while vacating their parental prison. But he came up with an addition to this old scheme: armed with an oscillating fan, a piece of garden hose, and a trash bag, he was able to have the lump in his bed mimic someone breathing. Then, with his apparatus in place, he sneaked out the window to the top of the prison building, where he had created a wooden bridge to the next building, from where he would jump over the fence and escape. But as he traversed his wooden savior, it broke, and he ended up stuck between the two buildings. Guards were finally alerted early in the morning when they heard someone knocking on one of the prison doors. Essentially, the prisoner had locked himself out of his own lockup. Obviously he is now watched more closely.

It's unfortunate, but we, the general citizenry, wash our hands of a convict once he or she is put away, believing that justice has been served. But it doesn't end there. Kris, Tee, and investigators like them all across the country spend their days listening in on phone conversations, interviewing prostitutes, and talking to gangbangers, investigating not only crime on the inside but also crime that is being orchestrated *from* the inside. It's a terrible reality, but all kinds of crime continue on—head bashings and stabbings on the inside, and harassments and killings on the outside. Unfortunately, that's the way the world is and always will be.

• • •

The next day, we caught back up with Sergeant Eric Rish at the St. Louis County Sheriff's Department within the city limits of

Duluth. He had arranged for us to look at the only ROV (remotely operated vehicle) owned and operated by a law enforcement agency in the country. An ROV is a mini-submarine, very similar to the ones used by National Geographic and the Discovery Channel to visit unreachable underwater locations such as the wreck of the *Titanic*. Homeland Security dollars have allowed many departments to purchase obscure and often irrelevant high-end pieces of equipment, and one could argue that this ROV falls into that category. Duluth is not a port city metropolis that terrorists are seeking out. However, Minnesota, the land of 10,000 lakes (actually 11,000, but that's not as catchy on a license plate), has a real need for this type of technology. Too many Minnesotans, under their own volition or with the help of others, often find their way to the bottom of one of the thousands of chilly lakes.

These underwater law enforcement cowboys, armed with their little sub, are pioneering the use of these aquatic pieces of equipment. Recently, New York City investigators finally decided that they too needed some of these subs to look under the boats that enter their harbor, and they asked the St. Louis County team to come and train them in using these machines. In this small circle of underwater investigation, these guys are well known—so much so that they were also contacted to assist on the Natalee Holloway case in Aruba. Investigators there hoped beyond all hope that an ROV might catch a glimpse of poor Natalee somewhere in the murky depths of the ocean. The St. Louis County investigators declined, however, because too much time had elapsed by then, and they knew their involvement would unfortunately be frivolous.

Underwater crime scene investigation is in its infancy. A lot of what is studied, including how bodies move in the water and how they decompose, is mostly conjecture. For instance, whenever you hear about someone falling into water, the experts come out and pontificate on where to begin the search for the body. Invariably, the thought is that "they move with the current, so we'd better look downstream." Then the body isn't found. Psychics show up pointing in all directions, while others clamor for a pig to be killed and tossed into the water to see where it ends up. But drowning is a very violent death. A victim will brutally thrash about, struggling for air, and a dead pig, believe it or not, cannot mimic that movement.

Almost always, a body will be found very near the point of entry. More often than not, when a body is *not* found near the point of entry, eyewitness error is to blame because the person pointed to an incorrect location. The trauma of seeing someone falling into and getting lost in a body of water is hard on the memory. The general rule of thumb is that a body will drift only about one foot horizontally for every foot it falls vertically in the water. There, the body will fall to the bottom and remain—at least for a while.

As a submerged body decomposes, it fills with gas, just as it will on land. In water, these phases of filling with gas have come to be known as *reflotation intervals*. The first interval is when the bacteria in the digestive tract cause the abdomen to extend and fill with gases (the bloat stage). This traditionally occurs between twenty-four and seventy-two hours after death. During this interval, the body will bob to the surface, float with the current awhile, and then, if undisturbed, sink back to the bottom until the second interval. The second interval occurs when the bacteria in other parts of the body (the tissues, muscles, etc.) begin to give off gases. Once this occurs, the body will typically start to float again. But none of this is an exact guide. Many variables go into these calculations, including the victim's last meal, the temperature and depth of the water, and even the body mass index we all love so much—meaning that fat people float more readily and are more likely to be found than skinny people are. Just another thing to keep in mind as you pull into the drive-through at Mickey D's.

The traditional means of underwater body recovery, and the way it is still done nearly everywhere today, is simply known as *drag and dive*. That is, get a boat, throw out a hook, and drag the bottom of the water. At the same time, divers go into the water and look around. Submerged bodies are never able to be recovered in "position found," as at a normal crime scene, because they have been disturbed during their discovery and recovery. Yet with an ROV, for the first time it's possible to find a body undisturbed.

• • •

The guys in St. Louis County had set up all of their equipment for us, their ROV and their sonar, in the conference room to let us observe them. Then they fired up a laptop computer and showed us tapes of something we'd never before seen—an actual body recovery by an ROV.

Wintertime in Minnesota means playtime on the lakes. And it is not much different from playtime in sunny Florida. But whereas Floridians drive onto their beaches to go fishing, Minnesotans drive right onto their frozen lakes and cut holes in the ice to fish. And instead of piloting Sea-Doos, they drive their snowmobiles all around the frozen waters. But the danger in Minnesota is exponentially worse. A couple of years ago, some guys put inner tubes around their waists and decided to go snowmobiling on a semifrozen lake. Unfortunately, one of

St. Louis County Sheriff's Office, Minnesota, ROV Team.
HALLCOX & WELCH, LLC

the guys fell through the ice, slid right out of his inner tube, and sank to the bottom to die. We watched the screen in awe as the mini-sub lit up the dark lake and showed the unlucky snow-mobiler dead, in "position found." The team had decided not to send their divers into the subzero waters, but instead used the clamp arm on the ROV to grab the body and hoist it to the surface. Again, we watched as the ROV moved into position, clasped hold of the snowmobiler's coat, and began pulling the man from the water. It was the first and only time so far that a body has ever been recovered by an ROV.

The surface has only been scratched about what can be done about crime scenes underwater. With the price of under-water technologies dropping (the equipment originally cost roughly $100,000) and the ever-present danger that exists in our country seemingly increasing, this field will soon explode with research and development. For now, though, these guys are as good as it gets.

The next morning, on the eve of the blizzard of '07, Eric picked us up to visit the Duluth Police Department, see some old friends, and talk about some of their cases. Duluth has sent four crime scene investigators through the forensic program, including Eric, so we were also able to visit with another foren-sic academy graduate, Lieutenant Kerry Kolodge.

Kolodge had had an interesting case not long after he graduated from our program. In July 2005, a call came in to the Duluth Police Department regarding a violent assault. The victim, Deliena Lamberton, had been severely beaten and subsequently taken to the hospital by her boyfriend, Edward Bergren. All indications were that the assault had even continued while en route to the emergency room. Kerry ultimately worked the scene, using the knowledge he had acquired in bloodstain pattern analysis to assess the directionality of the blood in the Ford F-150 truck where the assault occurred. "Either I was right on or way off," Kerry said, regarding his interpretation of the bloodstains found at the scene. His conclusion conflicted with the suspect's story.

"He claimed that his girlfriend went out one way, and the blood spatter evidence proved otherwise," Kerry told us as the wind began to whistle through the crevices of the old Duluth Police Department structure. In court testimony, Kolodge had educated the jury on forensic details such as height and directionality of bloodstains. The only thing he could not do was physically string the stains and come up with an area of convergence because of the truck's curved roof. Kerry consulted with Jeff Gurvis, one of the best bloodstain pattern experts in the country. "[He] told me not to worry about stringing a curved surface," Kerry said. Stringing a curved surface to calculate the area of convergence is a tough proposition left up to the most experienced analysts, and Kolodge had enough evidence without having to take on that challenge.

In the end, the defense brought in an expert from Florida who had nothing contradictory to say to Kerry's conclusion. The only question that was asked of the lieutenant was, "Have you ever witnessed anybody who was knocked unconscious standing on their feet?"—a perplexing question, especially when it is the only one asked. Kerry thought a minute and responded resolutely, "Not without some help." And with that, the jury deliberated and came back with a verdict of guilty. Edward Bergren was sentenced to 158 months for his violent attack on his girlfriend.

After we chatted with Kerry for a little while longer, catching up on old times, it was time for him to go back to work. We all said our good-byes and laughed a little as Kerry overaccentuated his "oo's" and "aye's." If it is possible, Kerry sounds even more Duluthian than Eric.

As Kerry vanished down the stairs, Eric grabbed the large three-ring binder that dominated the conference table and turned it toward us. "If we'd had an ROV back then, you know, we might have found Schrieffer sooner," Eric trumpeted, after our conversation with Kerry. Through the windows, we could see the snow just beginning outside, signaling the official start to what would become the blizzard of '07. Erik Schrieffer was a wannabe biker who went missing not long after he moved into the Hog Pen—a bar-slash-house-slash-biker-garage. At first, this case was nothing unusual. "These guys get drunk and crawl away or do something bad and run off to Mexico, never to be seen again," Lieutenant Ron Leino, another CSI with the Duluth Police Department, said as we thumbed through the case file. Leino had been one of the lead investigators in the case. And because bikers are not known for loose lips, no one at the police department expected much to come of it.

. . .

Several days after Erik Schrieffer went missing in January 2001, with the case fast becoming cold, investigators got a break when two eyewitnesses came forward to talk about the events they had seen at the Hog Pen. The fellow bikers, Herb and Charlie, said that Erik and another biker, Joseph Wehmanen, had gotten into a dispute over something about "living in Arizona." Nobody knew the specifics of the argument, but it grew more intense, with Wehmanen eventually accusing Schrieffer of being a narc. The two men spilled out into the street in front of the Hog Pen and fought, Wehmanen getting the best of Schrieffer, leaving him hunched over in the alley as Joseph went to his truck. And that's when the unthinkable happened. Wehmanen floored his truck and ran over Schrieffer, then hit reverse and backed up over him, and then rammed the truck back into drive and ran over him yet again, dragging him more than eighty yards in the process. The two witnesses said that at that point Wehmanen got out of his truck, threw Schrieffer into the back, and sped away. That's all they knew, and after their one conversation with the police, neither Herb nor Charlie was ever seen or heard from again.

Investigators were sent to examine the supposed scene of the crime, several days and several snows later, hoping to find some evidence of what had transpired. As the team scoured the area, one of the investigators noticed a reddish spot in the snow. Not knowing for sure but assuming it was blood, the team decided to do an excavation of the snowy area, just as they would if exhuming a body from a grave. After excavating down several inches, the investigators found a layer of blood, lots of blood, in a large swath, permeating underneath the snow. In order to collect the bloody snow evidence for analysis, ingenious investigators used foam cups and coffee filters as their forensic collection kits. The bloody snow was scooped up and its contents were put into a coffee filter set on top of a cup, thus filtering out the liquid as it melted and separating the blood from the snow. The blood that collected on the filter was eventually sent to the lab for DNA analysis. After the area was excavated and all of the blood revealed, the investigators then called in the medical examiner, who determined that even without a body, the amount of blood lost was sufficient enough to rule that a homicide had taken place. Erik Schrieffer was no longer thought to be missing; he was now presumed to have been murdered, and Joseph Wehmanen probably knew something about it.

Joseph Wehmanen was arrested on suspicion of murder, and his truck was seized and sent to the lab for analysis. Investigators were initially thrilled to collect the truck for the laboratory investigators, hoping that it might contain blood evidence. Earlier in the week, investigators had been called to a car wash where lots of blood was found being washed down one of the drains. Thinking their suspect might have taken his truck there to clean it up, they rushed to the location, but the blood they found was animal. It was hunting season, and animal blood would be found in many trucks in Duluth. Someone must have pulled into the car wash to wash out a fresh kill. Wehmanen, of course, had nothing to say about anything. Unfortunately, after three months of examination by the lab, neither did his truck. The lab couldn't find a trace of anything human or from a human—blood, hair, skin, clothing fibers, nothing. With Wehmanen still not talking and with no tangible evidence against him, investigators were desperate. One theory was that Wehmanen might have disposed of Schrieffer's body via an ice hole out at Joseph's friend's ice-fishing house (in Minnesota, icehouses are considered dwellings akin to mobile homes), but unfortunately the investigators did not even have enough evidence to get a search warrant for the fishing house. They could

The icehouse where police searched for Erik Schrieffer.

not hold Wehmanen indefinitely, and prosecutors would not prosecute him without something more than just conjecture to pin on him. Could Wehmanen be innocent?

With nowhere else to turn, the investigators decided to take a look at Wehmanen's truck themselves. They culled the truck, top to bottom, inside and out, and just like the lab initially found nothing. They crawled into the back of the truck, through the camper top, searching every crack and crevice. Still nothing. Then one of the investigators happened to look behind a piece of the camper top frame that supported the roof. And there it was: blood that had been splashed up behind the aluminum frame of the camper top, as if someone had sprayed a hose trying to clean something up. Still, it wasn't a tremendous amount of evidence.

The investigators decided, without even testing the blood to see whose it was (or whether it was even human), to inform Wehmanen's lawyer of what they had discovered and what their next move would be—to prosecute his client for murder. The lawyer and Wehmanen immediately decided to plead guilty to second-degree murder. Without a body or a lot of evidence, the prosecutor had little choice. As part of the plea deal, Wehmanen agreed to tell the investigators what had happened, at least his version of events, as well as where Schrieffer's body was, if he knew. Wehmanen was ushered to the St. Louis County district attorney's office right away, where he immediately began his testimony, even before the plea had been officially entered into the system.

The investigators interviewed Wehmanen at length about the events that unfolded on that night in January. Joseph Wehmanen was first read his rights, and then he began his conversation with the investigators. For the most part, the early portion of his testimony correlated with what the eyewitnesses had told the police. He and Schrieffer had fought over something about Arizona, they had spilled out of the house and into the street, and he had gotten the best of Schrieffer. But that's where the similarities ended. Wehmanen then told a tale far different than the witnesses had, one much more bizarrely philanthropic. Supposedly, Erik Schrieffer had pulled a gun on Wehmanen, and one of the bystanders had grabbed it from him and handed it to Wehmanen, telling him to "kill Schrieffer." Wehmanen, however, said he'd wanted no part of it, claiming that he'd responded, "I'm not going to shoot him." Instead, he said he unloaded the gun and put the bullets in his pocket, then handed it back to the person who had grabbed it from Schrieffer. He then claimed to have simply gotten into his truck and driven toward home, but noticed after a considerable distance that his truck wasn't steering very well. So he got out, looked under and all around the truck, and saw that he must have somehow *accidentally* run over Schrieffer, whose body had gotten hung up on the steering mechanism underneath the car. Wehmanen claimed that he'd pulled Schrieffer out from under the truck and "gave him a few breaths and chest compressions," attempting to resuscitate him. Wehmanen continued, "I decided then and there that, ah, since he wasn't breathing you know, that I had a better chance of probably helping him than they [Herb and Charlie] did by calling [911], so I put him in the back of my pickup truck." He tossed Schrieffer's body into the back of his truck and drove off in the direction of the hospital. Unfortunately, this is where his phony lifesaving heroics ended.

Wehmanen ultimately decided that he couldn't risk dropping off Schrieffer at the hospital because he might have to spend the night in jail for what it would have looked like he had done. So he drove to his mother's house instead, to do what clearly doctors would also have done for a person in Schrieffer's condition: strip him of all of his clothing; lay his body out on a tarp; steal three hundred dollars out of his clothes; and, as a last-ditch effort to save his life, smash his face in with a cinder block.

Wehmanen admitted to smashing Schrieffer's face several times with that cinder block. When asked by the investigators why he did it, he replied, "I figured I was going to prison and I was angry." They believe the contrary; they think Schrieffer was still alive, and Wehmanen was finishing him off. But no one will ever know for sure why he committed that last act of violence.

Wehmanen continued his heroic actions by tying window counterweights to Schrieffer's body, placing him into an army sleeping bag, and binding the whole macabre package with copper wire. Before he threw Schrieffer back into his truck, he also took some more cinder blocks and an ice drill, tools he would need to dispose of Schrieffer's body once and for all at the bottom of the river.

Wehmanen *did* know where Schrieffer's body was; he had always known. And the police's theory had been correct: Wehmanen had dumped Erik Schrieffer's body into an ice-fishing hole down from his friend's icehouse. "I was getting a little nervous," Wehmanen told investigators, because on the day after he killed Schrieffer he was planning to put his body into the water, but divers had been out looking around the icehouse. Therefore, he simply went back out to where his friend's house was, drilled a few small holes in the ice, smashed through the ice with the cinder block, and dropped Schrieffer's body into the St. Louis River.

Wehmanen then (as seems to be the modus operandi for all

Divers entering the frozen water, hoping to find the body of Erik Schrieffer.

THUNDER SNOW, AYE

criminals who kill and drive trucks) pressure-washed his truck over and over, making it spic-and-span—except for the blood he left in the camper top that eventually forced him to plead guilty and confess to what he had done. The prosecutors, armed with only a little splashed blood and no body, got the best sentence that they could, which was eight years. And he ended up where else but in the Stillwater prison. We'd bumped into him just two days before in the chow line.

Months later, with the summer thaw, Erik Schrieffer's body was eventually found on the Wisconsin side of the St. Louis River. This was only days after the sheriff's department had dragged the bottom of the river with hooks, pre-ROV style, and Lieutenant Ron Leino is still pissed off that Schrieffer's body washed up on the Wisconsin side of the river, seemingly taunting Duluth. "We loosened him up," he told us. Schrieffer's body had probably been lodged in some debris, and the dragging probably *did* loosen him up, his secondary reflotation interval causing him to move downstream with the current into Wisconsin. Among the throng in attendance for the dragging had been a handcuffed Joseph Wehmanen, who had given the investigators the starting point for the search. "Eight years, I don't feel I deserve that personally," Wehmanen told them. "Maybe manslaughter, possibly." If the investigators had retrieved the body before having to make a deal, he would most likely have gotten much more than the eight years. And with his confession, it is clear that he deserved to serve much longer. If a case like this happens around Duluth again, you can bet the ROV will play a huge role in the

The authors, Jarrett and Amy, standing in the middle of the frozen St. Louis River, near where Erik Schrieffer's body was dumped.
HALLCOX & WELCH, LLC

investigation. But until that time, it will continue to patrol the frozen underworld in search of unfortunate souls who find their way to the bottom of the frozen waterways in Minnesota—those who are weighted down with cement blocks and those who are not.

. . .

On our last day in Duluth, the day after the blizzard, with all schools closed and most of the roads too, Sergeant Eric Rish braved the weather to pick up us two lowly stragglers, with empty stomachs and day-old waffle burps. We drove around a bit as best we could, looking for something to eat, reminiscing about the academy and our friendship, and eventually ending up back at the station. We talk often to Eric, checking in with him from time to time, if for nothing more than to see how the weather is. But we knew something about Eric that we had never discussed with him before. Eric is a cancer survivor, non-Hodgkin's lymphoma.

As we sat at Eric's minimalist desk, snow permeating all around the windowsill, we clicked on a tape recorder and began our questions. "How has cancer changed you?" we asked tentatively, as if we shouldn't be prying into such a personal part of his life. In typical Eric fashion, a small tear slipped out of his left eye. He dabbed it with his thumb. We'd seen this before in him, back when he'd flown to Knoxville to tell the feds about his experience at the CSI School and what it meant to him and the City of Duluth. "I don't let things bother me," Eric said matter-of-factly. "One day, I finish a half-marathon and that night while I'm in bed I reach down and feel around my stomach and feel something the size of a block of Velveeta. I didn't feel bad; I just knew that it wasn't right." Eventually, after Eric endured eight horrible sessions of chemotherapy, his cancer went into remission.

We then shifted gears, asking him how he had found out about the academy in the first place. "We got a fax about the training," Eric told us. Fax blasting is a traditional means of recruiting cops for training. Many law enforcement agencies still don't have e-mail, and not just small departments—the

CSIs in New York City don't have working e-mail either. "Then we had a case where a graduate from Tennessee came to town on an investigation, and we talked about the academy." Around the same time Eric had received the fax from us, NFA graduate Tim Williams, from the Gatlinburg, Tennessee, police department, had come to Minnesota on the tail of a suspected murderer who had fled to Duluth. (The suspect had never bothered to change cars, and it was eventually found in the Home Depot parking lot where the suspect was then working.) While in town, Tim had talked to Eric about the academy.

"How did you get into this awful business in the first place?" we asked Eric, winding down our conversation. "Three words," he said: "the Congdon murders." The Congdon murders were dubbed the "trial of the century" in Minnesota. The case is a strange and convoluted tale of Marjorie Congdon and her husband, Roger Caldwell. Marjorie was the adopted daughter of Elisabeth Congdon, heir to a taconite fortune in Duluth. In 1977, Marjorie was suspected of having conspired with her husband to kill her partially paralyzed mother and her nurse, though she was ultimately found not guilty, and Roger pleaded guilty as part of a deal to have his sentence reduced to time served. In 1982, while in high school, Eric had heard one of the investigators talk about the case and the fingerprint evidence that had led to Caldwell's arrest. Even though the fingerprint evidence against Roger Caldwell proved to be erroneous, it nevertheless sparked Eric's interest in forensics. He was hooked from that moment on and chose policing as his career path. Though he has been promoted out of the day-to-day minutiae of the unit, he still champions forensic training, sending as many Duluth investigators as possible through the NFA program.

With our visit to Duluth over, we clicked the tape player off and prepared to leave, with hopes of catching a flight from Minneapolis, which had received considerably less snow. Driving the two-hour journey, we discussed the cold and the snow, and laughed about a picture Eric's wife, Kris, had shown us of two young boys sweating in a traditional (i.e., nude) Finnish sauna. Eric, of course, had been one of the boys. Eric's mother is a full-blooded Finn and had passed on the tradition to her son. "For Christ's sake, you didn't have to show that," Eric had exclaimed to Kris as we sprayed asparagus from the hotdish we were eating. Like all good Finns, Eric uses the sauna regularly to combat stress and decompress from life's worries. We know Eric well and know that deep down, regardless of what he might say, he does let things bother him, stressing about them day and night because he's a good officer, a damn good officer, and has great aspirations to one day be chief of the town in which he has worked all of his life. And we know that when he meditates in the heat, he thinks about his cancer, his wife, and his kids. Kris had told us, again with that one tear streaming down Eric's face, about how they had found out his cancer was in remission. Their daughter had "wished" it away around Christmas time, throwing a penny into a wishing well at a local mall. That same day, the call had come from the hospital telling them that his cancer was gone. In typical childlike fashion, the daughter was nonchalant about the information, telling her parents that she'd already known it was gone because she had just "wished it away." And when we think of Duluth, the snow, the ROV, the root beer, and the Rishes, we wish for Eric's cancer to continue to stay away, too.

4

Divining Intervention

LYNCHBURG POLICE DEPARTMENT, VIRGINIA

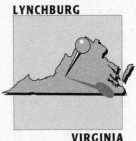

LYNCHBURG

VIRGINIA

Lynchburg, Virginia—the fifth largest city in the state—is unique in that it doesn't lie within a county. Instead, Lynchburg is surrounded by five counties, and is almost at the geographical center of Virginia. In its early days, Lynchburg was home to the largest Quaker population in America, but most of the Quakers abandoned Lynchburg in the early 1800s in opposition to the slavery that was happening at the time. Founded in 1786, Lynchburg was named for John Lynch, who owned a ferry service allowing people access to the other side of the James River. Mr. Lynch also put up the first bridge across the river, which eventually replaced his own ferry system. The James River was a major source of economic importance to Lynchburg, transporting tobacco and other items on shallow boats called *batteaus*, which were so important to Lynchburg that even today the city hosts an annual Batteau Festival. The police department has 202 employees.

Robbery. Assault. Vandalism. Grand theft auto. Sounds like the rap sheet of a hardened criminal, doesn't it? Well, it's not. It's the unofficial rap sheet of a cop—one of the most notorious graduates of our crime scene program, Bobby Moore from the Lynchburg, Virginia, police department. Bobby Moore spent his ten weeks at the National Forensic Academy working hard and studying hard, but playing even harder. We had no idea what we had gotten ourselves into when he arrived with all of our information already written down on a sheet of paper: birth dates, home addresses, Social Security numbers—when we met, he was already screwing with us. He partied and pranked us day in and day out as soon as class began. None of the staff of the school were safe. With the help of his fellow student cronies, we were, over the course of ten weeks, abducted from our vehicles, chased at high rates of speed, crime-scene-taped, and Silly Stringed. Our houses were rolled with toilet paper; our yards were vandalized with every Garage Sale sign, For Sale sign, and Lost Dog reward sign within a twenty-mile radius; and our doorknobs were strategically wiped down with Vicks VapoRub—a gift that keeps on giving, well into the night. If he hadn't already been a cop, we might have considered calling one.

As a matter of fact, we should have never even met Bobby in the first place. As a native Virginian, he shouldn't have been attending the school in Knoxville, Tennessee. Virginia is the only other state in the country with a forensic training program for crime scene investigators, and although its academy is open only to Virginians, it's free to the officer's department—if he or she can get a slot. When the time came for Bobby to go through the program, he discovered he'd been put on a waiting list that was more than a year long. Bobby is what we call in the South a "shit stirrer," and the fact that the Virginia academy wouldn't let him into its program didn't sit well with him. So he found our CSI training school in Knoxville; persuaded his chief to let him come to Tennessee; and, for the first time in history, someone left Virginia to be forensically trained in the art of crime scene investigation elsewhere. Since that time, three other investigators have followed his lead. This has caused quite a stir at the Virginia academy, not to mention a curriculum change. Needless to say, they are not that happy with Bobby. Good thing for us he is a shit stirrer.

"Hell, all they do all day long is sit in the classroom and jabber," Bobby claimed of the Virginia academy, as he revved up his Taurus police car. "They can't compare to what you guys are doing down there, and they know it," he continued. Bobby speaks with a wonderful antebellum drawl. He was taking us on a tour of Lynchburg, where he has lived and worked all of his life. Lynchburg, Virginia, is a quintessential Civil War town, located on the banks of the James River. Its location made it an essential transportation and supply hub for the confederates. Modern-day Lynchburg is known for basically two things: Liberty College, home to Jerry Falwell's ministry, and the tallest water fountain east of the Mississippi River. This water fountain, a water pump donated to the city from an old construction site, sprays tannic-acid-colored water hundreds of feet into the air in a fine stream. It looks more like a burst water main than a water fountain.

Bobby's law enforcement career began simply enough in the Virginia corrections system as a jailer, which had two prerequisites: a high school education and size. Bobby is a big and intimidating fellow, and with his diploma in hand, he was hired on the spot. Here is where he honed his craft—not in law enforcement practices per se, but in his ribald sense of humor. And with a literally captive audience, he practiced night and day.

Now imagine how you would feel if you were lying in a jail-cell bunk, sound asleep in the middle of the night, when all of a sudden this big corrections officer busts into the room with a flashlight, nervously scrambling to shine it under the bunk. Imagine, then, him doing this in several cells, not saying a word. The inmates would of course get restless, demanding to know "what the hell was going on." Then, without having uttered a single word during the commotion, Bobby, just before shutting the door behind him for the night, would say straight-faced: "Got a report that a python had gotten loose," and slam the door for good after finishing the sentence.

Believe it or not, deep down inside Big Bobby's tough outer shell lies the heart of an extremely good guy, and if you survive all of the bullshit that his big ol' mouth puts out, you might just get lucky enough to find it. Just as long as you're not a prisoner on his watch.

· · ·

We had come to Lynchburg to help Detective Bobby Moore and the rest of his gang look for some human remains that were thought to be part of a cold case dating back to 1989. In 1995, a skull had been found near the entrance to Blackwater Creek Park, which, coincidentally, is located almost directly below (down an extremely deep decline off a cliff) the house where the missing person from the cold case in question once lived. This was where we would begin our search, in the hopes of finding more remains.

On the morning of our search, we met Bobby and the other CSIs at the Lynchburg Police Department, housed in one half of the First Methodist Church of Lynchburg, which was erected in 1815. The other half of the church is condemned; it's falling in on itself and is too dangerous to occupy or worship in. Bobby's group consisted of a ragtag bunch who, though not dedicated to a crime scene unit, all include crime scene investigation as

The tunnel inside Blackwater Creek Park, where the possible remains of Lloyd Floyd Thomas were found.

HALLCOX & WELCH, LLC

part of their duties. One of these guys, John Romano, another graduate of our program, is unflatteringly called "Monkey" because he indubitably looks exactly like Curious George. Every crime scene unit has a whipping boy, and in Lynchburg, Monkey is theirs. When we arrived and were introduced to the group, we said hello to everyone and "Hi, John," to our former student. Nobody, absolutely nobody, in the unit knew who we were talking about. They had no earthly idea who "John" was. Monkey had become the only name by which anyone knew him.

To assist with our search for the remains, we had brought with us a set of body divining rods, similar to the ones Dr.

Arpad Vass has demonstrated for the forensic school at the Body Farm. The use and effectiveness of these rods is extremely controversial—just mentioning them in our first book, *Bodies We've Buried*, has led to our being bombarded by e-mails and vilified in chat rooms and blogs by those whom we shall call by their Latin scientific name, *Nothingus betterus todoerus*. All we did was simply mention that Dr. Vass showed how these rods *seem* to work. No tax dollars are involved, and the demonstration isn't even done during classroom time. We still contend that it's an astounding demonstration predicated on scientific research.

How it is hypothesized to work is like this: bone has piezo-electrical properties when it is under pressure. This means that, theoretically, buried bones may emit electrical waves that stream upward from their location. If they are not blocked or redirected by roots, concrete, or anything else that might be in their way, these waves are thought to interact with Earth's natural electromagnetic field. Thus, if one walks over a buried person with the divining rods, the disruption of the piezoelectric waves may cause the rods to move or cross. Divining or "dowsing" for water has been done for thousands of years. It has even been successfully used in situations where modern scientific equipment failed. So why not do the same with bone?

Some kooks even challenged us and Dr. Vass to take a Million Dollar Challenge and prove, once and for all, that divining for bodies using the *ideomotor effect* was a hoax. (The ideomotor effect is defined as involuntary movements caused by the mind. A good example of this would be the supposed movement of the pointer of a Ouija board by a person's mind.) It is impossible to prove to some people that we went to the moon if they don't want to believe it. The same is true for divining. If you have convinced yourself that you do not want to believe it, then it doesn't matter what we say; you'll never be convinced. Thus, we respectfully declined their challenge, told them to go bother someone else, and blocked them forever from our e-mail system.

We, along with Bobby, Monkey, our divining rods, and the rest of the team, arrived at the entrance to Blackwater Creek Park, which is hundreds of acres of very wooded, very rural, very hilly, and very rocky terrain. Trying to find human remains—better yet, trying to find *anything* in this area—with only eight people is an unbelievably daunting task, to say the least. Where do you even start on a cold case, an almost twenty-year-old cold case no less, with virtually no leads?

. . .

Back in 1989, a missing-person call had come in to the police department regarding a Lloyd Floyd Thomas, from Thomas's estranged wife, Thelle. Thelle and Lloyd had been separated for about eight years, and although Thelle had not permanently lived at the residence in nearly a decade, she still came by on a regular basis to take care of Lloyd. She told investigators that when she arrived at Lloyd's house on the day he went missing, the place was a mess, with furniture knocked over, a cigar burning in the ashtray, and Lloyd's glasses sitting on the table. Funny thing was, Lloyd didn't smoke, and he never went anywhere without his glasses. Even more mysterious, Lloyd's medications had been left behind in the house as well. Lloyd, an African American man in his sixties, had a bad heart and had been susceptible to seizures ever since a motorcycle accident nearly thirty years earlier. He couldn't afford to miss even a single dose of his medicine. Before investigators arrived, Thelle had unwisely decided to tidy up the house a bit and had cleaned up the crime scene, righting the table and chairs and other items that had been disturbed. Luckily, she remembered how things had been, and later returned the room to the disarray in which she had originally found it. Investigators took six photos and collected one bottle of brandy and another undetermined bottle of alcohol for fingerprints. That's it. Pictures of a re-created crime scene and two bottles. That was all the physical evidence they had to go on. Twenty years ago, this was a pretty standard practice for crime scene investigation. And because there was no such thing as DNA testing at the time, no one bothered to collect and package the cigar. Back then, most leads were predicated on whatever information could be garnered from interviews or statements from key witnesses. And indeed, about a month into this investigation, a key witness came forward.

Kevin Parsons, owner of the Save-Mor Furniture Store in Lynchburg, informed investigators about a story that one of his delivery employees, George Morton—Thelle Thomas's boyfriend—had been telling about the missing Lloyd Thomas. Parsons told the investigators that Morton claimed not only that he had killed Lloyd, but that Thelle had been in on it too. George Morton was a habitual offender and a dangerous man with a long rap sheet. Parsons came to the police because Morton had physically attacked him over a supposed debt. He'd become so violent that Parsons had had to pepper-spray him in the face to get him off. He had supposedly threatened to kill Parsons if he said anything about Lloyd's disappearance. Though Parsons wanted no one to know he had informed police about the incident, investigators discovered that he had been bragging about his working with the police to his friends. Police use and abuse snitches, and they know better than to ever trust one. Parsons's obvious enjoyment of his role had made investigators leery of his being a truthful witness. Nonetheless, they brought in Thelle and questioned her about her relationship with Morton and her supposed involvement in the killing of Lloyd Floyd Thomas.

The interrogation of Thelle didn't bring a whole lot of new information to light. She told investigators that five days had passed before she reported Lloyd missing to the police, and that she'd been to the house each of those five days, cleaning up the disarray that she had originally found. She also admitted that Lloyd didn't know that she was living with George—even though she'd been living with him from the very moment she'd left Lloyd eight years previously. The only piece of interesting information that came out of the interview was the fact that she had kept up a life insurance policy on Lloyd for years, even after she left him. An interesting bit of information, but nothing damning. Ultimately, the interrogation didn't bring any useful information to light, and Parson's story, though still believed by many, was not enough to make an arrest.

Over the course of the days, weeks, and months that passed after Lloyd's disappearance, several leads came in to the police department, none eventually going anywhere. They were all dead ends. People claimed to have seen Thomas everywhere—alive at his favorite "nip" joints, walking down the street, shacking up with some woman somewhere else in town, and even supposedly found dead by some kids behind an old hospital. The Lynchburg investigators ran down each and every one of the leads, interviewing people and searching the places where he was "last seen." Thelle even told investigators a month after Lloyd disappeared that someone had tried to enter the house with a key, because one day she'd found a padlock opened, and she and Lloyd were purported to have the only two keys. But once again, nothing came of these leads, and with no new credible information, the case went cold.

• • •

"Found him!" an elated Detective Moore yelled to all of us just off the bike path, near the mouth of the old train tunnel that defines the park, just seconds after beginning our search. Of course, he was being Bobby, and he had found nothing, though for a split second everyone thought he had. Serious

Bobby made an appearance for a few moments to give us all a briefing on how we would conduct our search. "Tiny said they came down through the tunnel and made an immediate left," Bobby informed the group. "Tiny" was the nickname of one of the retired investigators on the case. Back in 1991, two years after anything had been done on the case, a mysterious drunk had appeared in the back parking lot of the Lynchburg police station, screaming and crying "that he had killed Lloyd" and "couldn't get his face out of his dreams." He went on to explain to the now-growing number of officers who had gathered in the back of the police department that Lloyd Floyd Thomas's body was in Blackwater Creek Park, just through the tunnel, buried at the base of a big tree right off a dirt trail near the old railroad tracks. Investigators immediately gathered up the old drunk and drove to Blackwater Creek Park, hoping to find Lloyd, but though they searched and searched the area back in 1991, they found nothing. Still, that was where we would begin our first search of the day.

"A big tree" is not much of a lead, especially in a heavily wooded park. It's even less of a lead seventeen years after someone goes missing. But armed with our meager amount of information, we began our descent down the hill to what was presumably the original path that the drunk had mentioned. Bobby went his own way, up a very steep hill, toward Lloyd's old house. Only minutes into our investigation, many of the group began discussing what we would be having for lunch. Others poked fun at our brand of witchcraft as we sauntered through the woods armed with our divining rods, fashioned from coat hangers and tubing from yesterday's dry cleaning. Part of the process for using the rods is having the opportunity to walk slowly and smoothly, feeling for the interruption in Earth's magnetic field. But as we found out, that's nearly impossible walking downhill through leaves and mud. We chose the largest trees in the vicinity to conduct our dowsing search, slowly, steadily. No Lloyd.

The group scattered about the hillside, kicking over a leaf

John Romano, an investigator with the Lynchburg Police Department, trying our divining rods to search for bones.
HALLCOX & WELCH, LLC

here, a rotten tree stump there, overwhelmed by the prospect of looking all over the park for two-decades-old human remains. Boredom rolled in quickly, and as is customary with cops, with boredom came the joking. From Uncle Fester impressions to an uncanny rendition of Billy Bob Thornton's character in the movie *Sling Blade*, the ribbing continued, laughs echoing throughout the tunnel. Then, all of a sudden, at the zenith of our goofing around, Bobby found a bone.

. . .

After the 1991 alcohol-induced rant about the whereabouts of Lloyd Thomas, the case went dormant again for four more

Bobby Moore, of the Lynchburg Police Department, giving the team instructions on the search.
HALLCOX & WELCH, LLC

125

years. That is, until a skull found its way to the middle of the park entrance. Some bicyclists discovered the skull as they rode through the park toward the tunnel, on the opposite side from where investigators had searched back in 1991.

Cadaver dogs were brought in to the area to sniff out other possible places where human remains might lie dormant. The use of cadaver dogs is a curious undertaking. Some people swear by them; others, not so much. Trainers from across the country bring their dogs to the Body Farm in Knoxville to train. But every dog, be it a trained cadaver dog or your pet Rover, can smell evidence of human remains at the Body Farm—that's no test. Dr. Vass once did some informal research on a few dogs who could supposedly detect human bones buried deep within the earth. The results were mixed, to say the least. Part of the reason cadaver dogs have fallen out of favor is because of one renowned handler named Sandra Anderson, who pleaded guilty to five felony charges, including falsifying and concealing material facts from law enforcement officials, obstruction of justice, and lying to law enforcement officials. In other words, she would plant bones and other evidence stained with her own blood for her dog to find at crime scenes where police were searching for missing individuals who were presumed to be in the area. It was a horrible thing to do, and she was sentenced to twenty-one months in prison and ordered to pay $14,500 in restitution to several law enforcement agencies.

Though no other remains were found back then, the dogs had hit on a couple of "areas of interest"—places where decomposing remains might be or might have been. This was the area where we found ourselves, up on a ridgetop.

"Found him," Bobby again yelled, his voice echoing through the ravine. Indeed, he had really found a bone, one as green as a gourd. Alas, there was no doubt that the bone was animal, probably from a piece of meat bought at the grocery store. "Butcher marks," Bobby said as we looked at the bone. "Probably just junk from somebody's old campsite." We were no closer to finding Lloyd Floyd Thomas—that is, unless Lloyd was a rump roast from the local grocer.

• • •

The skull that had been found back in 1995 was sent to the National Museum of Natural History, part of the illustrious Smithsonian Institution, for examination by Dr. Doug Owsley. Dr. Owsley is one of the dozens of Dr. Bill Bass's prize pupils who dot the country, analyzing human remains. Though the exact numbers are not known, Dr. Bass is credited with being responsible for having taught at least half of all forensic anthropologists working throughout the world today. This incredible group forms the unique nexus between the new, modern-day forensic anthropologist and the scientifically trained crime scene investigator. Their impact can be felt all across the country. From the U.S. Army Central Identification Laboratory in Hawaii to the Smithsonian Institution in Washington, D.C., Dr. Bass's students continue to make an impact everywhere in helping to solve the mysteries left behind from human remains.

Dr. Owsley, whose work encompasses a wide range of interesting cases including the analysis of human remains from the first American settlement in Jamestown and the macabre and butchered bones left behind by Jeffrey Dahmer, received the skull from Lynchburg investigators in April 1995. In his report back to the investigators, Dr. Owsley concluded that the partial skull was from an African American male, at least fifty years old but probably older. This determination was acquired through statistical comparisons with other known specimens, which, over time, have been able to provide enough information to generate a database of measurements against which to compare samples. However, the skull found in Virginia was missing significant portions, particularly the mandible and the mandibular teeth. Unfortunately, without more bones, Dr. Owsley's ultimate analysis was inconclusive, and the report stated that a positive identification was impossible.

In spite of this, the Federal Bureau of Investigation, using photographs of Lloyd Floyd Thomas, created a computer-aided superimposition of the skull and the photographs. Dr. Owsley determined that the general shape of the cranium was "a good match," making several observations of similarity, including upper facial height, eye sockets, brow ridges, and what was said to be one of the most striking comparisons, the "moderately prominent glabella and depressed nasal root" (in layman's terms, the space between the eyebrows and the distance from the cheekbones to the nose). The final analysis of all of the compiled data: a high probability that the skull was Lloyd Floyd Thomas's.

Though the Smithsonian's analysis was interesting, it ultimately provided little boost to the investigation, and again the case went cold. The investigators who had first looked for Lloyd Floyd Thomas began to retire, passing their old relics of cases gone by to a younger generation of eager investigators. One of these new investigators was John Pelletier. In 2003, Investigator Pelletier took what remained of the case and began to organize it methodically to see what evidence remained in the inventory, what case notes still existed, what interview notes remained, and so on. Cold cases are not like wine—most do not improve with age. Pelletier didn't have a lot to go on. A few eight-by-ten photographs, some case files (others were missing), a brandy bottle, two latent prints lifted from that bottle—essentially the same pathetic evidence from fifteen years earlier, plus the skull and teeth, which were still at the Smithsonian.

But by 2003, new advances in forensic technology and capabilities had emerged, particularly the evolution of DNA analysis that could help the Lynchburg investigators garner new information. Pelletier decided to send the latent lifts, some of the teeth, and the skull to a forensic laboratory in Roanoke, Virginia, for DNA analysis of the evidence. Analysis of DNA evidence, particularly from a cold case, has become a crapshoot, to say the least. The serious backlog that is crippling our country's crime labs is reaching near-catastrophic proportions. It is similar to the last scene in the movie *Raiders of the Lost Ark*, in which the Ark of the Covenant is stored in an unimaginably large and very full warehouse for "later" analysis. We've seen container after container of DNA simply sitting on refrigerator shelves all across the country, awaiting analysis—some even in household refrigerators, in jars with sticky circular rings left on the bottom from months and years of condensation. By the time the analysts have time to get around to it, be it weeks, months, years, or even decades later, in some tragic cases, the evidence may be misplaced or lost or destroyed or simply no longer cared about. In this case, the Lynchburg investigators even struggled to get comparison swabs from Lloyd Thomas's living siblings. Some people are just suspicious of being called out of the blue to submit to having a giant cotton swab crammed into their mouths, collecting epithelial cells for a later comparison to a brother who has been gone for more than fifteen years—a brother whom they weren't even that close to in the first place. However, Lloyd's brother did eventually give a buccal swab for comparison to the skull's DNA.

Investigator Pelletier was persistent and thorough in his endeavor to resolve some part of the case, even if it was only to verify conclusively that the skull indeed belonged to Lloyd Floyd Thomas. And by persistent, we mean he bugged the hell out of the DNA scientists at the Virginia lab. In 2006, eighteen months after Pelletier had sent the items to be examined (the skull, the teeth, the brandy bottle, the latent lifts off the bottle, and the buccal swab from Lloyd's brother), the scientists finally analyzed the evidence. They isolated DNA from a tooth from the skull as well as from the fingerprints off the brandy bottle. But it was a weak profile. They also analyzed the buccal swab from Lloyd's brother, and though the samples from the tooth and from the brother had similarities, they were common across many people and had too few similarities to draw any conclusions. This was particularly true in 2004 when the evidence was sent. The only hope now was to do a mitochondrial DNA comparison.

Mitochondrial DNA analysis, even in 2008, is a highly specialized technique and one that is not easily or inexpensively obtained. There are only four regional mitochondrial DNA labs in the United States, and their backlog is roughly two years long—give or take. Private labs can do the analysis much faster, but the price is steep, running anywhere from two to five thousand dollars per test. And with police budgets tighter than they've ever been, that's money most departments cannot afford. Lynchburg is one of those departments. Though the resourceful Pelletier has had some conversations about striking a deal to get more DNA analyzed, for now the mitochondrial analysis will have to wait.

· · ·

After about eight hours of searching the hills and ravines for Lloyd, we finally called it a day. It was starting to drizzle, ahead of a massive cold front that had the meteorologists already talking about the possibility of snow later in the week. Lloyd Floyd Thomas would not be found on our search, and quite frankly, unless someone stumbles headfirst by accident into the rest of his remains, he probably never will. He could even still be alive; who knows? He would be eighty-one years old in 2009. We gathered our supplies, our divining rods, our green bones, and loaded everything back into the crime scene vans. Bobby locked the gate to Blackwater Creek Park behind us as we left Lloyd's supposed final resting place. For us, it would be the last time setting foot in this park. But for the investigators, the search may never end. It is still an open investigation to this day, with Pelletier attempting to arrange for the mitochondrial analysis and Bobby chasing leads like those from the drunken guy who'd claimed he'd killed Thomas. They've even arranged to go back into the house and process the scene for cleaned-up or faint traces of blood. It's a long shot at best. The sad thing is, the only potential suspect who was ever developed, George Morton, is now dead. They will probably never solve the crime, but hopefully one day they'll get a break and find Lloyd Floyd Thomas.

Back at the partially condemned church, also known as the Lynchburg Police Department, we gathered in the basement at the mini–crime scene lab with Bobby. The lab is very compact, but it has a fuming chamber and a few other forensic accoutrements that make analysis of minor evidence relatively easy. "Now, how do those damn things work?" Bobby asked, referring to the divining rods in that wonderful Virginian accent. He hadn't had the opportunity to witness Dr. Vass conducting this experiment in person. "Is he an alien?" Bobby asked us, joking.

"No, he's from Jersey," we told Bobby, laughing. We get that question all the time about Dr. Arpad Vass because of his wide-ranging intelligence on a myriad of topics—not to mention his stint at Roswell that he can't talk about. Frankly, sometimes we also wonder if he might be from Mars, mainly because we've never met anyone here on Earth as smart as he is.

Bobby tried out our homemade divining rods on the bones we'd found. We had constructed our rods using a hanger from the dry cleaner's, because dry-cleaning hangers like the ones that hold freshly pressed pants come with a round, hollow, cardboard tube on the hanging part of the hanger. All we did was simply cut the long portion of the hanger in half and remove the hollow cardboard tube (there now being two halves). The metal pieces were bent into the shape of an L and inserted into the straight cardboard pieces. The cardboard is the part of the rod that you hold, allowing the metal part to move about freely. We laid one of the bones in the middle of the floor and handed Bobby the rods. Back and forth he walked, slowly, holding his arms steady, walking right up to the bone, holding his outstretched arms over the bone. Nothing. He repeated it from the other direction. Again, nothing. "You sure Arpad's damn things work?" Bobby asked.

"They're not Arpad's. We made 'em," we told Bobby.

"I'll be damned," he yelled, faking anger as we laughed. "You drive all the way up here, and you two make the rods? You don't even bring the real set?" Maybe we were looking for "divining intervention" here in your "police church," we told him, tongue in cheek. "Whatever," he responded, flinging our rods into the air and walking past us in that typical Bobby Moore way of telling us that we were done here. And we were.

The next day we met Bobby at his other office, upstairs in the investigations side of the police department. The office was simply a large, open room with wooden floors and wooden desks arranged to get as many workspaces in there as possible. The brass of the unit had actual walls surrounding their sparse office space. Bobby is not only a crime scene investigator; he is a detective as well. The initials *CSI* are misleading, because individuals who work crime scenes don't typically investigate anything. They simply process the scene, draw no conclusions, and turn over the investigation to a detective. It's just another misnomer that is portrayed on television. However, though Bobby can process a scene, he spends most of his time investigating crime. On days when he is not dusting a fingerprint or stringing a bloodstain, he is shaking down leads.

"We're gonna knock on some doors today," Bobby growled as he grabbed his clipboard from his desk. A few days before we arrived in Lynchburg, some boys had broken a plate glass window in a local auto store. A security camera poorly captured the event, making identifying suspects a tough proposition. But as luck would have it, one of the kids *was* identified; and Bobby, based on a conversation with the suspect, was going to try to corral more of the players involved.

We left the police department in Bobby's Taurus and headed just up the hill to a residence not more than a mile from the station. Bobby pulled up right in front of the residence and parked on the street. "This ought to be interesting," he crooned as we exited the car. Within just a few steps up the paved sidewalk that led to the front door, we could hear the pounding of many sets of feet on hardwood floors, scrambling about the house in all directions. With all of the commotion going on, Bobby continued up the walkway, right up to the door, as we followed directly behind. On reaching the door, Bobby knocked three times, very hard, and took a step to the side of the door. We came to a halt like two rubes, directly in front of the door. "Yeah, that's where I'd stand if I wanted to get shot," Bobby said sarcastically. We immediately shuffled to the left, where Bobby stood, never having thought of "getting shot" as a possibility.

After more knocking, several "just a minutes" yelled from the other side of the door, and an endless stream of onlookers peeking from behind the curtains, someone finally opened the door. The person answering the door was an adult female, presumably the mother of the child in question, though apparently none of the ten to twelve boys roaming the house, peeking from behind doors, and looking down on us from the top of a staircase were hers. Bobby explained the situation as the woman yawned and stared off into space, uninterested in anything Bobby was saying. Ten minutes later, we were gone. "Do you ever worry about getting shot?" we asked as we nervously walked back to the car with our backs to the house. "No," Bobby said stoutly, "and once you do, you can no longer be an effective cop."

Bobby continued chasing down leads, with the same scenario playing out over and over: the running, the knocking, the waiting, the conversation with an unconcerned female, the mean looks, and all the rest. None of the boys were home on this day, and by noon, Bobby had exhausted all of his leads. "Do you ever get frustrated?" we asked as we headed back to the car the last time. "They'll turn up," Bobby said confidently. Then, all of a sudden, he frantically checked his cell phone for the time. "Oh hell, its lunchtime," he exclaimed. "Let's eat."

We and Bobby headed to an old sandwich shop called the Yellow Sub, where he'd been eating his whole life, just minutes from the house he grew up in. The hole-in-the-wall sandwich shop was very busy, but the savantlike owner knew everyone by name and exactly what he or she wanted to eat. We were the only ones in the place who had to place an order. Of course, everyone knew Bobby, from softball or from church or from the police department or just from being Bobby. "You're famous," we teased as we waited on our subs. In fact, we had been kidding him about that for years, ever since he'd been interviewed by *Popular Science* magazine right after graduating from our program. "Yeah, yeah, more like infamous," he replied, turning around to shake hands with someone from his church. Everyone knew Bobby Moore; it was like eating lunch with the Lynchburg Elvis.

Just before Bobby had attended the academy, he'd worked a case in which the victim, Loretta Napier, had been shot at close range and was found sitting upright on the floor. But what Bobby and the other investigators saw at the crime scene didn't seem to add up, and Bobby never really felt he had a good handle on how the murder had occurred—that is, until he came through the academy. When Bobby got back home, he went to the prosecutors, who were considering going after Napier's boyfriend, and was able to use his newfound knowledge to explain to them how everything had happened. "I could see the whole thing play out in front of me," he told the *Popular Science* reporter. With Bobby's new analysis as evidence, the boyfriend pleaded guilty to second-degree murder. "I guess I learned the most about bloodstain at the academy," Bobby said, chewing through his usual sub. "I guess I use that the most." That's probably true with most of the graduates of our program. Bloodstain pattern analysis is the Holy Grail of crime scene investigation training.

We finished our sandwiches and got a tour of the historical part of Lynchburg, culminating with a drive through the Old City Cemetery, hugely popular among Civil War buffs. It's two hundred years old and houses twenty thousand of Lynchburg's famous, infamous, and simply strange dead. We were especially intrigued by the history of the "appalling, terrific, bizarre, and unusual deaths" that dot the old cemetery. Of particular interest was the death of poor Parham Addams, who came to his unfortunate demise when his soda water machine exploded and left an imprint of his face in marble. We will certainly pay more attention to the "contents under pressure" warning on all those soft drink bottles.

With our history lesson complete, it was time to say good-bye to Bobby. We had a long drive ahead of us and a looming cold front coming from behind. Bobby gave us his typical bear hug, wishing us well on our journey. Detective Bobby Moore is the definition of "a character," and he has become a true living legend among all of the graduates who have graced our program. Every two years or so, graduates from all across the country gather back in Knoxville, Tennessee, to participate in the Biennial Alumni Retrainer, to learn new and cutting-edge techniques that are being taught, and to get as drunk as skunks. That's where Bobby has really become infamous. At the last event we had back in 2006, Bobby tried to steal our Hummer, and when that failed, he and seven other alumni crammed themselves into a Ford Taurus and spent the night at one of Knoxville's best haunts—a country-western bar called Cotton-Eyed Joe's. Unfortunately for the proprietors of the establishment, it was quarter beer night. They didn't turn much of a profit on that night. But come first thing the next morning, there was Bobby, looking fresh as a daisy. "I'm getting too old for this shit," he said as he scooped up some runny eggs from the breakfast buffet. He probably *is* getting too old for that stuff, but we hope he never changes.

5

Mamas, Let Your Babies Grow Up to Be Cowboys

TEXAS RANGERS

SAN ANTONIO

TEXAS

San Antonio is the second-largest city in Texas and one of the ten largest cities in the United States. It is the county seat of Bexar County; the city was founded in 1718, though Spanish explorers had been living there as early as 1691. San Antonio was the site of the infamous Battle of the Alamo, where Texans fought against the Mexican army for their independence; in 1968, it hosted the World's Fair, of which the Tower of the Americas is the only remnant still standing. The San Antonio River flows one story beneath the city, making the River Walk one of the city's most popular tourist areas. In 2006, the Texas Rangers were involved in some capacity with 886 murder cases throughout the state.

Very few things are left in the world that transcend time. Elephants and alligators are good examples, windows to a past that no longer exists. But even these living dinosaurs are dying out, and when they are gone, generations will simply wonder in awe about a time when they roamed Earth.

Human history has very few examples like these left. Most of us now walk upright, and less and less of us still wear powdered wigs. Yet scattered across the wild Texas terrain, hundreds of miles from nowhere, still roam 116 of the gun-toting endangered species called Texas Rangers.

The Texas Rangers can trace their ancestry back to 1823, when Stephen F. Austin commissioned ten men he referred to in his journals as "Rangers" to protect the Anglo settlements from the giant Karankawa Indians. Since that time, the Rangers have survived abolishment, Bonnie and Clyde, and even Texas governor Ann Richards.

When it comes to the Rangers and their unique brand of law enforcement, not much has changed since the saloon days of the Wild West. They are still the quintessential cowboys, with the boots, the hats, the ultradecorative handmade leather gun belts, the guns of their own choosing (ornate in every sense of the word), and, last but not least, the badges, which are made from a 1947 or 1948 Mexican cinco peso—a holdover from a time when Rangers had to make their own badges so they could be identified by the town marshal.

In the early days, Rangers were essentially provided nothing by the state (or the republic, as it was called back then). They were organized as a militia-type outfit, with each Ranger bringing with him his own horse, gun, and other necessary supplies as part of the deal. In modern Ranger times, the state does provide them with a few necessities, including a gun—though they are not required to use it. In keeping with their heritage, the Rangers can carry whatever gun they want, so long as it falls within a few parameters. They are the only outfit in the entire Texas Department of Public Safety not required to use the standard department-issue Sig Sauer.

Some places in America clamor for gun control, even to the point of pushing for legislation to stop police officers from carrying weapons. But not in Texas and certainly not with the Rangers. Their jurisdiction is the state, and their means are by whatever means necessary.

"They should have ironed him out right there," Ranger John Martin told us, with a sheepish grin as wide as the Rio

Grande Valley. To "iron someone out" is the euphemism many Rangers use in reference to shooting a bad guy. Martin was telling us a story about how he had persuaded a renegade truck driver to stop his rampage through the town. "He was running over troopers, and we weren't gonna have that," Martin said coyly, crossing his full quill ostrich boots up on top of his desk. These boots have seen many a crime scene and have been put through many a perp's door. "What did you do?" we asked, already assuming the answer. "I shot him," Martin said, as matter-of-factly as if he'd offered the driver a piece of candy.

That's the Texas Rangers in a nutshell. Try that anywhere else and a cop might get fired, or at least time off without pay and a lot of paperwork. But Ranger Martin was never even questioned. Texas Rangers have been empowered like no other law enforcement agency in the country.

We first met Ranger John Martin at Session VIII of the academy in 2004. During our customary meeting the Sunday night before the class begins, Martin was easily identifiable as the first person we'd ever had wear a cowboy hat to the event. He even kept his hat on during a burial exhumation, while working and digging in heavy, wet snow—the same snow our Minnesota investigator experienced. Since Martin's graduation from the program, we've had four other Rangers follow in his footsteps and have added two others as instructors.

We had come to San Antonio to visit Martin and his unique Ranger unit, UCIT (Unsolved Crimes Investigation Team).

UCIT was formed in 2002 after much politicking by a local influential family whose invalid patriarch had been erroneously accused of killing his wife. The case was a tragic example of shoddy police work, not to mention just plain stupidity.

• • •

The case was doomed from the initial call, considering that dispatch was informed that they should call "the meat-wagon" (a nickname for the coroner) because they had a "natural causes" death, even though the woman was naked from the waist down and had had her throat slit from earlobe to earlobe.

Eventually, the sheriff's department showed up and determined that it was a homicide. Yet after working the crime scene for less than two hours, they collected the body and packaged four cigarette butts as the only evidence in the case. They quickly decided that the husband was the perpetrator, even though he was bedridden when they arrived. "Hell, he had three days' worth of shit in his diaper," Martin explained to us. Despite the husband's having no blood on him and the lack of blood trails to where he lay, the sheriff's department's whole case was attributed to the invalid husband "acting" sicker than he really was. Eventually, they filed a case against him with the district attorney and considered the case closed.

The case remained unsolved for six years until the son, who had been working relentlessly to get somebody to listen to him about the case, finally got the attention of a victim advocate who got him a meeting with the Texas Rangers. The son told his story to Al Cuellar, the Texas Ranger who'd drawn the short straw, who read the case notes and looked at the crime scene photos. At the end of the conversation, Ranger Cuellar told the son something he had never heard from anyone but had wanted to hear for six years—his father did not kill his mother. Cuellar knew that the case was FUBAR (fucked up beyond all recognition), and that finding out who did kill his mother would be very tough if not virtually impossible. So he promised the son that he would devote one entire week to the case, dropping everything else. If nothing came out of that one week, then there was nothing more that he or the Texas Rangers could do.

Within a couple of days, Cuellar discovered that although a rape kit had been collected on the victim six years ago, it had never been processed. Every day rape kits are collected from victims, many of which are never sent to the lab for profiles. Even in today's modern forensic world, some people in law enforcement still look at the technology as if it's witchcraft. Without a profile, DNA cannot be run through the Combined DNA Index System (CODIS) for a possible match to another crime, but the backlog in laboratories and the huge caseload of investigators unfortunately puts the rape kit at a very low priority. However, once the kit was finally processed, although the DNA could not confirm who had committed the murder, it was able to exclude who didn't. The husband was exonerated and removed from the suspect list, though the case still remained unsolved.

BEHIND THE YELLOW TAPE

Six years of accusations were wiped away with only two days' worth of good police work. Cuellar would now be elbow deep into the case until he retired. Everyone considered him a great police officer, one of those investigators who lived and breathed the areas he worked, and who knew everybody in town. Some people just have a knack for investigating crime, and Cuellar was one of them. "This is one of those crimes where I bet you could throw a rock from the victim's house and hit the son of a bitch who did it," Cuellar said, about the case. He went into the neighborhood and resurrected the time frame, going door to door to ask the folks who lived in the community "who was the meanest no good son of a bitch who lived around here back then," when the murder happened. The answer for most was easy—Billy Sutherland. Billy Sutherland became a suspect and was coaxed into giving a DNA sample. But at this point in 1996, DNA technology was still evolving, and the test did not pinpoint him as the assailant, though it didn't rule him out either, as it had the husband. Of course, without any definitive evidence, no arrest could be made, and Cuellar, who was fast approaching retirement, turned the case over to Ranger John Martin. The case was a quagmire, but Martin was eventually able to confirm that Billy Sutherland was the killer through an advanced DNA test from a lab in North Carolina. (Oh, and the four cigarette butts? They were from the guys who'd originally worked the scene.) In the end, it was still hard to prosecute because everybody got their feelings hurt. "It was a pissing match," Martin said. Even in the face of DNA evidence that proved it impossible, some people were still holding on to the theory that the invalid man had killed his wife. Though Billy didn't get the sentence that he probably should have, justice was finally served. Solving the case was the impetus behind the creation of a dedicated cold-case unit, and thus UCIT was born.

. . .

The UCIT unit is composed of eight Texas Rangers dedicated full time to investigating cold cases, as well as serialized or unusual murders. The office is located in San Antonio in a non-descript strip mall, bookended by what just about everything in Texas is bookended by—a Whataburger fast-food restaurant on one side and a mom-and-pop Mexican joint on the other. This office contains the highest concentration of Texas Rangers anywhere in the state, except for the Department of Public Safety home office in Austin, where the bureaucratic "suits" reside. Other Rangers are spread throughout the state, most working alone covering nine county areas.

The offices at UCIT are very sparse and minimalistically decorated, save for a few pieces of cowboy paraphernalia. Ranger Martin's office is no different. He has only one "I love myself" tribute displayed in his office: his U.S. Air Force commendation for outstanding military service, served mostly in Guam as a military police officer. (We did, however, notice one other piece of John Martin regalia, pushed back on his bookshelf between the *DSM-IV* psychology text and another book titled *Practical Homicide Investigation Techniques*: the Class Leader Award presented to him by the staff for serving as the Session VIII class president at the NFA.) Martin has a lot of books crammed on his shelves, all dealing in one way or another with the psychological aspects of crime scene investigation. Martin is the Texas Rangers' one and only behavioral analyst, classically trained by the Federal Bureau of Investigation (FBI) and stationed at the UCIT unit to analyze criminal behaviors related to cold-case murder investigations.

Nearly all of the sixty-some-odd cold-case investigations that the unit is working on at any one time are truly the worst of the worst. Not necessarily *worst* in the way that the crime was committed, but in how the case was worked. We refer to these cases as the "cream of the crap."

"It's hard to work a cold case," John Martin began, a little preoccupied. On the day we arrived in San Antonio, he'd been busy on the Internet, requesting a custom-crafted gun to replace the one that had been stolen from his house just a few weeks before. In typical Ranger fashion, Martin worked his own crime scene, pissed off beyond belief that something like this had happened. God, Texas, women, children, and guns are the things most valued by Rangers, and we'll let you put them in the proper order. "I bet the son of a bitch who stole it is back across the Rio Grande Valley, laughing with his buddies as to what he did," Martin said, through gritted teeth, as he continued researching his gun. "But I found prints where he looked into the house and entered them into AFIS; one day, I'll get a hit." Martin had discovered one of the most common prints left at a scene—the karate chop print, which appears where a perp, usually a burglar, cups his hands around his eyes to look into a window, casing a place he wants to break into. Martin dusted and lifted these beautiful prints, and now, should the guy ever get caught, he'll have something to compare them to. We wish the perp luck. Never separate a Ranger from his gun; it just might land you in the chair.

"As I said earlier, it's hard to work a cold case," Martin started again, fidgeting over our recording our conversation. "Many agencies don't even still have any of the original evidence from the case." That's true of virtually all cold-case investigations. There are no specific rules or laws covering every type of evidence or how long it must be kept in storage. After twenty years, many agencies purge old evidence, not expecting that a piece of clothing or a sheet from a homicide may hold any further value. Then along came DNA analysis, a way to investigate the past, so to speak—but only if the evidence still exists.

"When you do get somewhere, few prosecutors even want to take on the case," Martin continued. "Then you have a jury pool where very few were even born when the case happened." Couple those circumstances with very little evidence, a few bad Polaroid photographs, some poorly written case notes, and you have a very difficult and unexciting case to prosecute.

Yet cold-case work, or *unsolved* case work, is all the rage in law enforcement right now. Every case is *unsolved* until it is *solved*, no matter how long the investigation takes. Most

Texas Ranger John Martin with one of his many cold-case files.
HALLCOX & WELCH, LLC

departments have always, either formally or informally, worked cold cases. However, in today's environment, many agencies are dedicating specific units to these cases, and thus, they compete for notoriety and, more importantly, funding. And funding is directly correlated to clearance rates. "When we started the unit," Martin began, "we wanted to have something to compare it to." So Martin and other Rangers called cold-case squads from across the country to see how they tracked their clearance rates. They found that some of the squads had extraordinarily high clearance rates compared to the others. "They were cooking the books," Martin claims, with a crooked smile. "They told us that they counted everything." And by *everything*, they even include theories on "whodunit." But although investigators may "know" who really committed the crime, that's not usually enough—an investigator must also be able to prove it with evidence, statements, and the like. From what John learned, several of the cold-case squads had simply counted theories about what they think they know, as well as what they can prove, in their number of closed cases. The Rangers in the UCIT unit count only what they can prove and resolve.

· · ·

One of the many downsides to theories, John says, is that "people get married to their pet theories and get plum mad when you pose another possibility." He'd had a case up in Round Rock, Texas, in which Christina Moore, three months pregnant, had been brutally murdered. The police were sure that what they were seeing at the crime scene meant only one thing—that her husband had done it. "Anytime you work with an opinion already formed, you are going to miss a lot," John said. The Round Rock police had asked him to take a look at the crime scene and, using his behavioral analyst training, give his opinion about the type of perpetrator who could have done it. "I believed that it was a sexual predator from the very beginning," John said, disagreeing entirely with the direction of the Round Rock Police Department's investigation. "They got really pissed off at my assessment." Behavioral analysis can be very polarizing, particularly when an investigator cannot keep his biases in check and clouds the investigation by formulating his own theories, differing from the behavior analyst's and rooted in feelings instead of facts. Despite this, behavioral analysis is a useful forensic tool.

The investigation into Christina Moore's death dragged on, going nowhere for more than a year, with the Round Rock Police Department still convinced that the husband was the killer. Things such as an overturned coffee cup and a dog covered in blood led them to formulate their theory on the husband. "If the husband had done it, then he was a genius," John said to us as he thumbed through his case files, referring to inconsistencies in behavior that he observed at the crime scene. "The gal had been attacked at the door," John pointed out. "A husband doesn't do that; he has access to the house." What it boiled down to for John was that rarely do people plan a killing out to a T—thinking ahead, staging things, husbands attacking from the outside, and so on—unless they are unusually gifted criminals. And other nuances of the scene, observations we won't give away here, indicated that it was a sexual homicide committed by someone other than the husband.

Then, in 2004, a woman came forward with new information on the case. Betty Johnson, sister-in-law to one Michael Moore (no relation to Christina), got mad at Michael one day and decided to tell the Round Rock Police Department that he had checks belonging to a Christina Moore. Moreover, Michael had given his wife a new set of wedding rings, which he claimed he had purchased from a man at a day-labor center. Funny thing was, Christina's rings had been missing; her husband had pictures of them for insurance purposes—and the rings Michael Moore had given his wife were a perfect match to the ones taken from Christina.

Other things connected Michael to the case as well, and he was eventually arrested, ultimately confessing to this crime and to another murder, and sentenced to life in prison. Thus, John's original theory was vindicated. "Did you get a call from the Round Rock Police Department when all this happened?" we asked, assuming that they would have called him back once the investigation concluded, especially because his original analysis proved correct. "Shiiiiitttt," was all John had to say in response to that question.

The next day, John made it his quest to keep us from eating at chain restaurants while we were in San Antonio. Fortunately for us, John's lovely and artistic wife had introduced him to a nice, frou-frou type of restaurant called the Guenther House. The Guenther House is the original home of the founding family of the Pioneer Flour Mills, and this eclectic house has been turned into a part museum/part kitschy restaurant, the kind of place where, John claims, "They'll make you put a pretty flower in your hair." Translation: It's a girly joint, though the food is really good.

At this lunch, we also hooked up with another academy graduate, Ranger Chance Collins. Chance is also stationed in San Antonio but with one of the traditional Ranger units, Company D. Your typical all-American good-looking guy, Chance is six feet, six inches tall and built like an athlete. He has a very intimidating presence, and as a result he is known to be great at getting confessions out of suspects. He is also lovingly referred to by other Rangers as a *chula*, or pretty boy. A few of these *chulas* are employed by the Rangers, and they traditionally get assigned all of the governor or presidential details because they look good on camera. So we, along with Ranger Martin and Ranger *Chula* Collins, arrived at the Guenther House, minus the flowers in our hair but attracting many a stare nonetheless.

The hostess led us to a small round metal table decorated

Texas Rangers John Martin and Chance Collins on the steps of the Bexar County Courthouse.

HALLCOX & WELCH, LLC

with decoupage flowers on the top, and we seated ourselves on filigreed iron chairs. It was the type of table you might see in the corner of an English garden—not the type where two gun-totin' Texas Rangers would usually be caught dead sitting. Most of the space was taken up by legs, elbows, and cowboy hats, but we made do.

"Any weird cases, Chance?" we asked, thumbing through the menu consisting of foods Rangers don't typically eat, such as crepes, hollandaise sauce, and marmalade. We could tell that Chance's wheels immediately began turning, deciding whether to pull our legs or tell us something for real. He chose, for the time being, a real story. "Yeah, I got this weird case," he began, digging at his front teeth with his customary toothpick. A body had been found over in some woods on an officer's piece of property. "Case goes to trial next week. Strangest part of the case was how the body had been messed with." Indeed, the body had already gone through the bloat-and-purge stage, releasing volatile fatty-acid fluids such as putrescine and cadaverine. "I was smelling his shorts," Chance said as John Martin gave him the crooked-eye. "I noticed his shorts smelled like decomp, and I thought it was strange." It *was* strange, particularly considering that the shorts were not found on the body but at least a hundred feet away. The body was also covered by new-looking, fresh tree branches—too new, considering the length of time that the body had been there. It appeared that someone had disturbed the body postmortem by placing the newly cut branches over it as a rudimentary camouflage. "When we caught the suspects, they confessed to going back to the body and removing the dead guy's shorts," Chance told us. The reason they gave was that they'd seen on the show *CSI* that they might have left finger-prints on the body, and also that bleach gets rid of all kinds of evidence. So they went back, removed the guy's shorts, and scrubbed him down with bleach. Perps learning from shows like *CSI* are becoming a common theme for real crime scene inves-tigators. It's another problem attributed to the CSI Effect: bad guys going that extra mile not to get caught, based on some-thing they've seen on television. Sometimes, thankfully, it leads to blunders, as in this case or in the John T. Snow case (see Chapter 2). But other times, it does not.

"By the time I came to the NFA, I had been a Ranger for seven years," John said later, as we walked back to our car after lunch. He chucked his cowboy hat into the backseat. "I felt like I had a pretty good handle on it. Then I got to the NFA and saw the quality of instruction, and it made me reflect back on some of the cases I had investigated over the years and how I could have done things better or differently. Not only did I recognize my own deficiencies, I recognized that my deficiencies were also the Rangers' deficiencies." John had laid the groundwork for other Rangers to come to the academy, and he even started a mini–crime scene school for the Rangers, building on many of the concepts that he learned at the NFA.

That's been a constant theme with virtually every graduate we have ever talked to. It's not that anyone was doing a bad job; that's certainly not the case. But there had never been a place specifically dedicated to the art of crime scene investigation, where CSIs could learn from other CSIs and practice their craft, developing new and innovative techniques. Not to mention the NFA's unique environment, far different from most other police training academies. "I've been around these little regional police academies in the state, where they've hired some retired police officer who thinks he knows it all," John told us as we drove around San Antonio. "What you get is a guy with one year of experience he's had twenty-five times over, and he's over there trying to teach new police officers, and completely closed-minded to anything that is outside his realm of knowledge and understanding. You guys impressed me right off the bat saying that you would never be satisfied with the way it is right now. I thought, wow, what a great attitude to have for any training program or educational endeavor, and these folks are going to be successful and make a big splash."

John's comments were very flattering, and they reflected what the NFA set out to do. We intentionally engineered the academy to be unlike traditional police-training venues. We had made a concerted effort to be different, to be more interactive. We wanted input, we wanted feedback, we were open to change, and we listened to everybody's opinion. These were not ideas readily accepted in the rigid, paramilitary, and very strict hierarchical police world. But they're concepts that are very conducive to learning.

The next day, we went with John and his lovely wife for a taste of San Antonio culture—Fiesta. Originally called the

Partygoers at Fiesta, a San Antonio celebration.
HALLCOX & WELCH, LLC

Fiesta San Jacinto, Fiesta is a ten-day celebration in honor of the heroes who died during the battles of the Alamo and San Jacinto. In modern times, Fiesta has morphed into a drunken fest with cheap taco bars and thousands of *cascarones*—colored empty eggshells filled with confetti. As we ate the Fiesta food, John talked about a recent cold case he'd investigated.

• • •

Back in October 1980, John Gough was shot and killed by his wife, Wanda, in what was determined to be an act of self-defense. But John's brother Fred had never believed the story and had tried unsuccessfully for years to get the case reopened.

Finally, after much persistence, the case landed in John's lap in May 2005.

"I could tell right away that it more than likely wasn't self-defense, as Wanda had described in her statement twenty-five years [earlier]," John said. He matched the wounds from the photos of the deceased to Wanda's original statement and was able to make out inconsistencies. "Where she says she shot her husband, and how, just didn't match with what I was seeing," John recalled. "So we went back to the house where the shooting had occurred." When they arrived, "we asked the owners if we could take a look around the house, and they let us in."

"There were turnip greens cookin' on the stove and Ray Charles playin' on the record player," John said, with a chuckle. "It was like we had stepped back in time." And sure enough, right where the shooting had occurred nearly twenty-five years earlier were a couple of poorly patched bullet holes, low to the floor, hidden behind a wardrobe. Again, more information pointed that [Wanda's] original statement didn't add up.

"I almost cringe when I hear the term *criminal profiling*," John said. "The way it has been portrayed in movies and television is not accurate. Criminal profiling or criminal behavioral analysis is simply a way to lend a behavioral perspective that traditional law enforcement training doesn't necessarily expose you to." Essentially, what a profiler does, broken down into its base components, is to try to look at a crime and think what happened, why did this happen from the offender's perspective, what role did the victim play, and who would have been motivated to do this. Simply stated, but a real art form in practice. John ultimately interviewed Wanda in 2006 about her husband's death. She hadn't had as much as a speeding ticket in twenty-five years, but within minutes, she confessed to having fabricated the whole self-defense story.

Ultimately, Wanda was indicted by the grand jury and arraigned in the Gregg County 124th District Court, where the trial was set to begin in early 2007. Nobody wanted to see this case go to court except for one person—John Gough's brother Fred. "The DA offered to plea the case, getting a guilty verdict, and [have] Wanda serve no time, maybe pay a dollar or something," John told us, over a huge piece of cheesecake. But Fred would have none of it. She was guilty and she would stand trial. And she did. Ranger Martin flew down and testified on the case, just as he was supposed to. He had garnered a complete confession from Wanda and had matched the evidence to corroborate her own incriminating statement. It was a slam-dunk case. And yet, "When the jury went back to deliberate, they came back with a verdict of not guilty," he said, shaking his head. *Not guilty.* That's how it goes in the world of cold cases. Solving one is a combination of good luck, hard work, and serendipity. And even when all of those things line up, the final decision is still left up to a jury.

• • •

John had arranged for us to take a helicopter ride in the Texas Department of Public Safety's very own helicopter the next morning. It flew all of the way in from headquarters just to take us up for a bird's-eye view of San Antonio. While we waited for the copter to arrive, we asked John whether there was a case that still haunted him. Indeed there was; there always is. "Yeah, I've got one," John said, taking a swig of Dr Pepper. "When I just joined the unit, this guy came in with a story about a murder in San Antonio that he knew something about. Most times, these stories go nowhere, but this one, well, it was interesting." It was interesting indeed. John's case came during all of the publicity that occurred when the unit was created. The guy was a walk-in off the street, seemingly a nut. But John dug around in the files of the San Antonio Police Department and found an unsolved murder that had occurred at nearly the exact time frame this guy was talking about.

"Did he get a lot of detail right?" we asked.

"No," John responded flatly. The street the murder had actually occurred on was one over from the one he had claimed, and the details weren't really any more accurate than what could have been read by anyone in the paper. But the guy had led John to an unsolved homicide, so he decided to try to work it. And he's never stopped working it. There was an unidentified suspect's DNA as part of the evidence, but that was about it. So John dove deep into the area, making contacts, trying to revive the details about the victim and the neighborhood.

"The vic was a good-looking real estate agent who was doing work on her house, so she had a lot of people coming in and out," John explained. "I even got a DNA profile from one of the construction guys who I thought could have done it, who was then living in Utah—it turned out not to be him. I've been all over the country getting DNA; I have no real leads. I even asked around the neighborhood, asking if there were any perverts who were known to peep around, and I found one, a young kid who would go around skinning his carrot looking into people's houses." But despite the potential lead, who admitted to being a peeping Tom, the swab came back negative. "I didn't think he'd done it anyway," John admitted. Nobody's DNA matched the suspect's, not even the guy who'd started the whole thing by coming in. Eventually, John polygraphed the guy, who failed the test miserably. "I didn't know what to think," he said as the roar of the helicopter began to hum through the hangar. "I even contacted the guy's wife, who said she knew all about her husband claiming he had intimate knowledge of that crime. I believe the guy is just a drug burnout who was around when the murder happened and absorbed some of the details; I don't think he had anything to do with it."

"Do you ever think you'll solve it?" we asked.

"Maybe," John shouted, over the roar of the rotors that had yet to come to a stop. "Maybe I'll get a hit in CODIS or something one day. But he could have died or been incarcerated before the DNA law went into effect for felons." John was referring to the thousands of convicts all across the country who were incarcerated before it was common practice to swab felons for DNA to be entered into the FBI's national DNA database

CODIS (Combined DNA Index System). "Texas passed a law, and we are going back and swabbing all felons," John told us, before we posed for our picture with the Ranger and the helicopter. "But with the backlog, it will be years and years before they are all submitted." Unfortunately, as wonderful as DNA evidence can be, it's worthless if it's not collected and analyzed. John may never solve this particular case, but he works on it, even if for just a little while, every month.

When we returned from our helicopter ride, it was off to another meal. John and his wife had made reservations for dinner at an off-the-beaten-path place named the Grey Moss Inn.

The authors, Jarrett and Amy, with Ranger John Martin (center)
in front of the Texas DPS helicopter.
HALLCOX & WELCH, LLC

The inn resides along the original stagecoach route that ran all the way from San Antonio, Texas, to San Diego, California, and has a deep and rich Texas history, complimented nicely by authentic Texas cuisine—meaning meat. Lots of meat. All kinds of animals were being roasted on a huge open fire at the inn. Vegetarians beware.

John had also invited some of the other Rangers and their families to dinner, including Chance Collins and Troy Wilson. Ranger Wilson is now an instructor at the NFA whom we originally met through John. Troy and another Ranger, Oscar Rivera (with whom we unfortunately didn't get a chance to visit on our trip) often teach crime scene mapping, showing CSIs how to sketch crime scenes on a computer.

The dinner was a nice change of pace, just time to relax, decompress, and laugh. "We ought to do this more often," John said, swirling his glass of wine at the head of the table. These guys and their families don't see as much of each other as one might think. This dinner was a quasi family reunion for them, and a chance for us to meet their wives and children.

After a huge meal was served to us by a wacky waitress, and with dessert on its way, John told a few tall tales about his days as a state trooper. "We had these ol' boys, and all they wanted to do was pull pranks," John said, with that all-too-familiar Texas grin. "These boys would do just about anything. One evening, getting toward dark, these two troopers happened on a car with a flat tire and a New York license plate. These poor folks were driving across country and were getting close to one of the reservations in the area frequented by out-of-towners—a.k.a. a tourist trap. The troopers pulled up behind and got out of their car. One of the guys went up to the group and asked them, did they know what they were doing and that they were driving through Indian country and that the Indians were on the warpath? Before the New Yorkers could answer, the other trooper turned his back to the group and pulled out both pistols and began firing wildly with both hands into the woods, screaming, "Here they come!" The poor New Yorkers nearly killed themselves speeding away, leaving their jack and three lug nuts behind. They had watched too many *Gunsmoke* reruns. We all sat there laughing and wiping tears away while John grinned proudly at the entertainment that he had provided. With stomachs full and sore from laughter, we all got up to leave, with hugs and handshakes all around on our last night in San Antonio.

But there was still more food to come in the morning. Every Friday morning in San Antonio, you will find a gathering of Texas Rangers eating breakfast at one of the local establishments named Las Chiladas. This breakfast meeting has become a tradition for the Rangers in San Antonio to come and eat, hang out, catch up, gossip, and talk. We arrived at Las Chiladas and were ushered back to the reserved table beneath the two wall hangers—purchased by the Rangers themselves—needed for hanging up all of the cowboy hats.

During breakfast, the Rangers chatted, talking a little about active cases, bouncing ideas off one another, most being

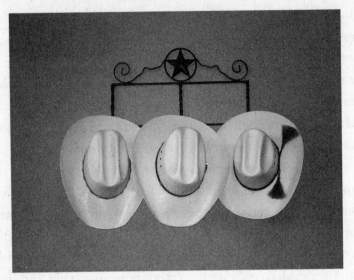

Texas Rangers' hats hanging on the wall during breakfast.
HALLCOX & WELCH, LLC

a little quieter than usual because there were two authors in the room. Eventually, though, they loosened up and started telling war stories: about murder, about drag queens, and about ghosts. Stories about how after thirty years, people who had gotten away with murder begin to lose sleep and begin telling others, because it eats at their very souls. John chimed in and said, "When you get a guy close, just reach in and touch him on the stomach, he'll tell it all."

After about an hour of talking and laughing about all of the crap that they see, John unloaded probably the best quote and the strangest story of the trip. "A policeman's badge is a front-row seat to the greatest show on Earth," he said, with a laugh. It sure seems that police officers deal with some of the most outrageous circumstances; at times, you just can't help but laugh, or at the very least let your mouth hang open, at the unbelievability of what you are hearing. "We had this case one time that was about the strangest thing I'd ever heard," John began, knowing he had captured our attention. When cops think something is strange or weird, look out.

"This ol' gal was crying, walking along the side of the road," John said, posturing to tell the story in the way only he can, "when this van pulled up and stopped next to her. There was a normal-looking, middle-class husband and wife in the van, both trying to console the girl. As the conversation continued, the husband got out of the van and walked around to the passenger side door, while his wife continued to talk to the girl. When the old boy got close, he shocked the girl with a Taser gun, opened the sliding door, shoved her in, cuffed her to an eyehook in the middle of the van, and drove off."

John continued. "They took this girl to a weird little house with no doors or windows, except for in the back of the house. They got her out of the van, stripped her naked, and threw a rope up over an exposed rafter inside the house and collared her around the neck. After they had tied the girl up with the rope, making sure she was secure, the old guy and the gal pushed up a dinner table next to the girl, stripped naked themselves, and sat down and commenced to eating spaghetti." At this point we're all listening to this with our mouths agape, just waiting for the punch line.

"The couple didn't talk much, the girl said. They just communicated with hand signals. At one point, she explained, the old boy popped his elbow up on the table, and held up the peace sign or the number two to his wife, who immediately jumped up and ran down the hallway. When she came back, she was carrying one of those hospital urinals and without missing a beat, hit her knees, crawled under the table, and crammed the ole boy's root down into the urinal, where he relieved himself. When he was done, she pulled the ole boy's root out, cleaned him off, crawled out from under the table, took the urinal back down the hallway, came back, sat down, and went back to eating spaghetti without saying a word." ("Ah shit," someone said.)

"She then said that when the couple finished eating, they pushed back from the table and untied her from the rafters and marched her down a hallway to nowhere. When they reached the end, the wife grabbed for the fake wall, revealing a hidden bedroom with an old mattress on the floor and another exposed rafter in the ceiling. They again tied her up, but allowed her enough slack to lie down. The wife then tossed her a book and told her to study it." The couple closed the wall back, went next door, and commenced, as John so eloquently explained, "whippin' and spurrin' and fuckin' like there was no tomorrow"—all night long. "The girl told us that the book was full of phrases used to say to your master," John said.

"When the next morning arrived, the girl told us that she was glad and surprised to be alive, so she decided to go along with what the book said, to try and survive, call him *master* and stuff like that. That morning, the wife put on clothes, went to the grocery store, and, at some point—the police later found out—went bowling, believe it or not. The ol' boy cleaned his rifle and put the girl on the vacuum, still naked and still tied up. After she had called him *master* a couple times, the ol' boy untied her and allowed her to vacuum freely while he continued to clean his gun."

"With every pass she made, she tried to get close to the sliding door that led out the back of the house. When she finally got close enough, she waited until he wasn't looking and dashed, buck naked, all ninety pounds of her, a quarter mile up the road to this old farmhouse. She rounded the driveway and literally busted through the back door, where this eighty-year-old lady was sitting having her morning coffee. She began yelling for the woman to call 911. The old lady did, at the same time clutching at her chest. At virtually the same time, the ol' naked boy rounded through the back entrance wearing nothing but his rifle. He threatened the old lady repeatedly, demanding she tell him where the girl was (she had hidden under some clothes in the closet). He scuttled about and found an old pair of pants that didn't fit, pulling them up to just barely on his hips.

"As he continued to threaten the old woman, the old lady's son and daughter-in-law arrived on scene to the chaos, and the ol' boy commenced to threatening them too, and still threatening to kill the old lady if she didn't tell him what he wanted to know."

John continued the story. "Unbelievably, and as if on cue, the sheriff's deputies showed up—all four of them—including the paper-pushing constable that nobody liked. Immediately, a standoff ensued as the guy, with his pants barely on his hips, yelled at the cops and they yelled back. The son decided to be a hero, going back to a chest of drawers and grabbing a .22 pistol. He ran to the back of the house where the standoff continued and fired a shot, missing the ol' boy completely. But the shot started World War III," John said, shaking his head.

"As the shooting began, one of the deputies had a clear line of sight on the ol' boy and fired all six of his bullets, missing him every time, and having no bullets remaining. Another deputy simply froze and cried, never drawing his weapon. The deputy sheriff was firing on the ol' boy from behind his cruiser door when the naked guy shot out the windshield and shot part of [the deputy's] finger off. The ol' boy, having wounded the deputy, came down from the porch to lay him out when the constable, the guy nobody even liked, went to his trunk, got a rifle, and shot the ol' boy square in the back, ending the whole scene."

"What happened?" we asked, with childlike wonder.

"Well," John said, "the old lady had a heart attack and eventually died in the hospital. So we worked the scene, collected the evidence, and prosecuted the wife who was part of the kidnapping. Ultimately, though she claimed she was a battered wife, she got forty years for what happened."

"What about the evidence?" we asked, laughing, already

expecting the answer. "We collected swings and dildos and homemade shit none of us had ever seen or heard of. We had no idea how some of it would be used or where most of it would even fit." Guess it is true what they say—everything *is* bigger in Texas. And with that, the boys grabbed their hats, paid their checks, said their good-byes, and set us off on the road to catch a plane in Houston.

. . .

Walking through the terminal at George Bush Intercontinental Airport, the fourth-largest airport in the United States and the sixth-largest in the world, we realized something—we stood out. We were decked out in our shorts and tennis shoes while all around us men and women alike wore cowboy hats and Wranglers. We had slipped through a portal, our very own *Twilight Zone*, where everything was different. But what do you expect from a state that had to write its own declaration of independence against another country, from a state that *was* another country, and from a state that prides itself on its gunslinging heritage? Different it is. And thank God for that. Where else would the concept of the Texas Rangers work except Texas? Nowhere. And it probably won't always work in Texas either. Some unthinking lawmaker will one day abolish this last vestige of another era of law enforcement that harks back, even if just a little, to Wyatt Earp and Doc Holliday. A time that everyone wishes he or she could be a part of—even if just for a few seconds. We were able to get that experience with the

Rangers, traveling back in time. No, we didn't ride on horses; instead we drove around in a Ford Taurus. And no, there were no *High Noon* shootouts in the middle of the street. But there were tips of the brim of the hat, "howdy ma'ams," and sippin' whiskey. Currently, the Rangers enjoy just about the best reputation they've ever had, for solving crimes and holding state officials' feet to the fire. One bright legislator, when an argument erupted over who should guard some sensitive data, told the rest of the representatives that the information should be given to the Rangers to watch over. When asked why, he simply stated that there were only two things in the world that he trusted—"God and the Texas Rangers." Amen to that.

6

CSI Frappuccino

SEATTLE POLICE DEPARTMENT, WASHINGTON

SEATTLE

WASHINGTON

Seattle, Washington, probably best known these days for Starbucks Coffee, was once known for its lumber and shipbuilding industries. Though Seattle was officially founded in 1851, archaeological evidence has shown that humans have been there since as early as 8000 B.C. The city is surrounded by natural beauty, bordered by Lake Washington and Puget Sound and surrounded by the Olympic Mountains to the west and the Cascade mountain ranges to the east. The city also sits atop an active geological fault known as the Seattle Fault, which was last active in 2001 when a magnitude-6.8 earthquake shook the city. Most people think of rain when they think of Seattle, but the average rainfall is actually one of the lowest in the country. The Seattle Police Department has 1,837 employees; in 2005, the Crime Scene Investigations Unit worked twenty-five murders within its jurisdiction.

Back in the sixties, Perry Como crooned that "the bluest skies you've ever seen are in Seattle." And it may be true to those who live and work in the magnificent Emerald City, though we're not sure how they even remember what color the sky *is*, considering the cloud cover that seems to always blanket the city. The city of Seattle, Washington, is sandwiched between two mountain chains—the Olympic Mountains to the west and the Cascades to the east—and it looks out across Puget Sound, where the warm waters of the Pacific Ocean keep the temperatures relatively mild year round. These waters and high mountains keep Seattle vested underneath a layer of marine clouds most of the time. But when the sun does shine and that wonderful blue sky comes into view, Seattle's remarkable natural wonders are revealed, including the breathtaking and usually snowcapped Mt. Rainier that seems to sit guard over the city. Yet contrary to popular belief, Seattle is not nearly the rainiest city in America—it's not even close. As a matter of fact, it usually doesn't even crack the top ten; Mobile, Alabama, takes the number one prize in that category. It is, however, the city that experiences the least amount of sunshine, the cloudiest city in America. This lack of sunshine has contributed to three things Seattle is best known for: serial killers, suicide, and coffee—three very different, yet uniquely related issues. This overtly cloudy area has produced one of the world's most notorious serial killers in one Gary Ridgway, better known as the Green River Killer, who admitted to killing forty-nine women in and around the Seattle area over the course of more than twenty years.

The cloudiness has also contributed to Seattle's being called by some the "Suicide Capital of the World," where dark days encourage depression, and the large number of bridges invite the depressed to jump off to their ultimate end. The city no longer even mentions suicides in the paper for fear of causing a copycat effect and tempting even more people to jump off bridges.

Lastly, Seattle is home to the ubiquitous Starbucks—the leading coffee retailer in the entire world. Within the city limits of Seattle are forty-four Starbucks stores, with dozens of other branches owned by the chain dotting various outlets throughout the city. No other city in America needs a pick-me-up like Seattle does, which helps explain why Starbucks and a host of other coffee vendors thrive side by side on virtually every street, serving java to the masses and hopefully helping to medicate those would-be serial killers and potential jumpers.

Unlike most other areas of the country, here in the Emerald City cops and crooks alike can agree on one thing: a good cup of joe. Invariably, crime scene photo after crime scene photo shows an easily identifiable white-and-green Starbucks cup—in *venti* size no less—somewhere in the background, lurking under tables, sitting on park benches, or in the hands of an investigator. So much coffee goes down the gullets of Seattle-ites that we began to think we should propose a forensic study titled *The Effects of Coffee on the Smell of Decomposing Flesh*, maybe even discovering a new chemical leeching from the body called javarine. But by our last day in Seattle, we found out that we no longer needed to conduct that study. Decomp still smells like decomp no matter how much coffee you drink.

We had arrived after our cross-country flight just in time to catch NFA graduate Detective Mark Hanf testifying on the stand about a 2006 case—a gang-related shooting. Kevin Monday, the defendant in the case, had gotten into an altercation that turned into a shooting in the middle of the street, where he fired wildly, hitting two people in a car and one on the street. The person shot on the street, Francisco Green, ultimately died of his wounds. Ten fired cartridge casings were among the evidence collected at the crime scene.

The case was a homicide, but since a fatal shooting had occurred inside the halls of the King County Courthouse in 1995, the entrances and exits of the public courtroom were highly regulated. No one could enter or leave until the judge granted a recess. After sitting outside the courtroom for several

Crime scene photo from the shooting at Pioneer Square
in Seattle, Washington.

minutes, chatting with another NFA graduate, Detective Brian Stampfl, we finally entered the courtroom.

Trial court, real honest-to-goodness trial court, is, well, boring as hell. Atticus Finch, poignantly speaking to a jury and saving Tom Robinson from his demise, is nowhere in sight. We watched our pasty-skinned friend Mark, wearing his trademark fanny pack turned to the front, take sealed envelope after boring sealed envelope; cut it open, careful not to damage what was inside; and display the contents (in this case, fired cartridge casings) to the jury. Multiple cartridges had been collected at the scene, and according to good crime scene technique, each had been packaged in a separate container. After repeating this procedure numerous times, jurors and bailiffs alike were nodding off in their after-lunch coma. Starbucks should consider a kiosk in the courtroom.

Despite knowing that his life was hanging in the balance by what Mark was showing the jury, the defendant seemed even less interested in what was happening on the stand. (Of course, it might have had something to do with the fact that the entire chain of events had been caught on tape by a street musician who had left his camera on while he had been performing on the street.) The defendant appeared more focused on how he might flee the courtroom, gauging the guards, their guns, and the distance to the door. He sat next to his attorney, slowly turning his chair toward the door and nervously eyeing the guards. Then the anti-drama improved a bit when the prosecutor asked the court for permission to enter the judges' chambers and retrieve another piece of evidence. What he came back with was the passenger door off a Mazda, riddled with bullet holes. As the twelve men and women craned their necks to see the car door, Mark came down from the witness stand and educated the court on bullet trajectory, discussing each bullet entrance in depth.

Finally, after all of the evidence had been entered into the trial, it was the defense's turn to cross-examine Detective Hanf. "You don't actually do all of the stuff they do on the television show *CSI*," the defense attorney began asking Mark. On TV, he said, "They collect evidence, analyze it, and investigate the crime, so why do you call yourselves CSIs?" Mark smiled just a little because of our presence in the courtroom; we had had this very conversation about how invariably the defense's first course of action nowadays is to cast doubt by referring to the television show *CSI*. "We call ourselves crime scene investigators because we investigate crime scenes," the ever-introverted Mark answered, never making eye contact with the defense attorney. At that point, even the judge intervened, commenting tongue in cheek that the popular TV show likely stole the term *CSI* from police agencies. Everyone in the courtroom sort of chuckled, and the defense attorney's futile attempt at using the CSI Effect to create reasonable doubt in the minds of the jurors melted right before his eyes.

It had been three years since we had last visited Mark. On his return from Knoxville, Mark had organized a new mini–crime scene school, and we'd brought a bloodstain course to the Seattle Police Department as a kickoff. In 2003, Mark had come through the academy representing one of the largest cities in the United States that at the time did not have a dedicated crime scene unit. During his training at the academy, Mark realized that his department *needed* a dedicated crime scene unit to respond and bring consistency to the investigation of all violent crimes occurring within its jurisdiction. And then on TV one evening in 2006, we both caught a glimpse of a familiar stocky fellow in a white Tyvek suit working a crime scene being broadcast live on CNN. Mark and other NFA alumni, as well as future alumni, were all dressed up in their Michelin Man attire, working the largest and most horrific crime scene the city had seen in the last quarter century—dubbed the "Capitol Hill Massacre"—with their fully *dedicated* crime scene unit. What had once been an agency many years behind the curve was now benchmarking practices and sharing crime scene skills with agencies across the country. It goes to show that with the right person leading the charge, even in a bureaucracy, a lot can happen in just a few years.

Mark finally finished testifying for the day. The jurors were removed from the courtroom first, returning to their room in single file while the rest of us stood waiting for the judge to release us. Then, with the jurors safely tucked away behind closed doors, sheriff's deputies handcuffed the defendant and took him back to his cell. The jury never saw him brought in or taken out in handcuffs. Mark came down from the witness stand to greet us two tired and very weary travelers, and so with two sleepy out-of-towners on his hands, he was forced to take us to Starbucks for a pick-me-up. (Mark is an anomaly in this city—he doesn't drink coffee, never having acquired a taste for the stuff.) After a good Starbucks drink and a short drive back to our hotel, we crashed for the night, resting up for our first full day with the Seattle crime scene unit.

The next morning, or as we prefer to call it, the jet-lag-from-hell morning, we found our way down to the CSI Unit and the Police Support Facility of the Seattle Police Department. Seattle's new CSI Unit is centrally and wisely placed among the department's other forensic units (Latent Print Unit, Photo Lab, and Video Unit) as well as the Washington State Patrol Crime Laboratory. As championed by the city's highly regarded police chief, Chief Kerlikowske, the City of Seattle renovated—what else?—an old Starbucks packaging facility and turned it into one of the best forensic areas we had ever seen. This new building is well equipped, extraordinarily organized, and multifunctional, providing every opportunity to work virtually any type of case.

One of the most unique aspects of this complex is the vehicle processing bay—the envy of the Pacific Northwest. On average, one car per day arrives into this facility to be processed by either Seattle crime scene investigators or latent print examiners. It has room for dozens of cars, trucks, motor homes, boats, and just about anything that can be driven, floated, or flown. It even has a lift to transport many of these vehicles upstairs for long-term storage on more important cases. Touring the upstairs was similar to visiting one of those weird car museums, like the ones in Pigeon Forge, Tennessee, or Myrtle Beach, South Carolina, that display cars with their own names and reputations, or cars that Elvis owned or that Hank Williams, Sr., died in. Except here, Mark walked with us down each row, telling us the often terrible stories behind each car, including the one with the missing passenger side door, which was still propped up in the downtown Seattle courtroom as a reminder to the jurors (who eventually found Monday guilty of homicide and sentenced him to sixty-four years).

Some of the vehicles had been there for years, trace evi-

Seattle investigator Mark Hanf examining the car driven by
one of the victims from the Pioneer Square shooting.
HALLCOX & WELCH, LLC

dence already faded or covered up by a thin dust layer of sedi-
ment that had begun to collect on the exteriors. There were old
cars, new cars, foreign cars, domestic cars, hoopties, and clas-
sics—each with a unique yet tragic story to tell. In one corner
of the garage we even came upon a pleasure boat sitting cocked
to the side, looking strangely out of place. Mark told us the
story behind the boat: It had been involved in an accident with
another boat in which several people were hurt and one person
was violently killed. As we walked around the side of the boat,
we could still see the blood smeared across the bow—another

eerie reminder of how quickly and unexpectedly a life can be taken.

One of the CSIs who, by default, has become a sort of curator for the crime-car museum is Detective Kevin O'Keefe. Detective O'Keefe is one of those old, stereotypical homicide investigators found in every department. The guy has seen and done it all, lives on caffeine, and acts as if he hates just about everybody. That's Kevin. Only he acts as if he hates us just a little bit. Kevin spent nearly five years working on the Green River Task Force trying to catch Gary Ridgway back before DNA technology was all the rage. For months, after Ridgway's eventual capture, members of the task force, including Kevin, searched the Green River area weekend after weekend, along with other wooded clusters in and around Seattle, for the remains of Ridgway's victims. It took years to recover the pieces of the missing prostitutes that the Green River Killer had considered "throwaways." He would bury them in groups so he could drive by and relive the moment, but unfortunately he wasn't that bright (or maybe he was) and claimed to have forgotten where a lot of them were buried. A shackled Ridgway was brought out to an area where Kevin and others had cleared acres of brush looking for bits and pieces of these murdered girls. Many times, the guys, including Kevin, got ribbed, hearing, "Hey Kevin, come over; I've got some brush in my backyard you can clear." But over time, they were rewarded by finding at least some of the remains, though ultimately no one believes that they have all been accounted for.

As we continued touring the amazing facility, Mark took us to the unit's staging area. It was immaculately conceived and organized to the hilt—everything had a use and a place. And just like every other place we visited, ingenuity prevailed. Bureaucracies are wrought with a quagmire of impediments, written down in a compendium and usually guarded by a forked-tail person with big, red, pointy horns. Many of these "rules" stem from incidents that no one remembers and probably weren't big deals anyway. But there they are, on the books, harder to remove than an indigo tattoo. So the CSIs in Seattle improvised on many things, creatively acquiring and paying for items out of their own pockets to make their jobs easier and their performance better. Otherwise, they might still be working out of a scarcely supplied silver van.

Behind the gates and lockers and other organizational accoutrements hangs the CSI Unit's shoulder patch, designed by none other than Mark Hanf. It's just pinned there on a corkboard, without any fanfare (and without any real approval). The patch was created, displayed, worn, and traded proudly by the fledgling unit. The existence and acceptance of the patch by the police department is akin to a rite of passage, making the unit an officially accepted part of the agency.

Mark conceived the entire unit, creating a survey instrument for other large agencies across the United States in an effort to determine how their departments handled crime scenes. The Seattle CSI Unit's beginnings were auspicious, with the unit starting out on a six-month trial basis. Mark recruited seasoned

Investigator Mark Hanf shows off the Seattle Police Department's
well-stocked crime scene van.
HALLCOX & WELCH, LLC

veterans to the unit from among interested people from various detective units. He also put together the mini–crime scene investigator school and sent all of the new recruits through it over a period of a few months. The design of the unit was to get experienced investigators with an interest or a penchant for crime scene work to work in the newly formed unit. Many departments don't have this luxury when creating a crime scene unit, often putting unseasoned cops without much experience into either investigations or crime scene work. An even worse trend around the country is using civilian crime scene technicians who have little or no police experience whatsoever and a sum total of training from a one-hour videotape on how to dust for prints. This is not to say that civilians can't make excellent crime scene technicians; they most certainly can—as long as they have the requisite training and experience. But taking fresh college grads and putting them on the street is not the way to run a crime scene unit.

We have heard of several cases in which an untrained investigator made a leap in logic based on what was presumed to be the situation, relying on simple visual clues and statistical probability rather than on the evidence. For instance, victims of hypothermia can sometimes suffer heart attacks, tearing at their clothes and bare chests because of the pain. To an untrained investigator, it might look like a homicide. But someone with experience will know better. Suicides are another good example. It is a common belief that people who want to kill themselves won't stab themselves with knives. But they will, and they have. And in a few cases the suicidal person has begun with one knife, sawed at his throat, and then, unsatisfied with the results, moved on to a bigger and sharper knife to finish the job. Again, to an unseasoned investigator, several different blade marks on a victim's throat might look like foul play was involved, rather than self-inflicted wounds.

The group Mark amassed for the crime scene unit certainly had that crucial investigative experience. But some administrators of the Seattle Police Department didn't think the unit, regardless of their experience level, would be busy enough to last six months. Fortunately for Mark and the rest of the team—if unfortunately for Seattle's crime statistics—they couldn't have been more wrong. Nowadays, the unit is so busy not only with responding to crime scenes but also performing other administrative duties, such as public presentations and training, they can hardly keep up with all of the casework. And just as in all good bureaucracies, none of the original naysayers can be found. History has been rewritten, and now everybody claims to have always been in favor of the creation of the unit.

· · ·

The area known as Capitol Hill in Seattle is home to an eclectic mix that might be termed *counterculture*, with a large gay community, wannabe grunge rockers, and twenty-somethings dotting the historic sidewalks adjacent to magnificent mansions. It is the second most densely populated area in Seattle, with a very active night scene, including bathhouses, bars, and the occasional rave party. On March 25, 2006, the Capitol Hill Arts Club had been the scene for a special zombie-themed rave party titled "Better Off Undead." Partygoers had decked themselves out in pale makeup and squirted themselves with fake blood. After hours of waving glow sticks, playing with Hello Kitty dolls, sucking on pacifiers dipped in ecstasy, and lying around in "cuddle puddles" (groups of ravers lying around massaging each other), a crowd moved on to a nearby house popular with the goth crowd for an after-hours party. Ravers are a very friendly bunch and invite anyone and everyone to join in their festivities. Residents of the house had bumped into an unassuming guy at the rave and had unwittingly invited him back to the party. Little did they know that for some, it would be the last invitation they would ever extend.

The inconspicuous guy they had so graciously invited was named Kyle Aaron Huff. Kyle was a twenty-eight-year-old troubled transplant from Montana who had moved to Seattle in 2002. Here he expanded his level of discontent as an unemployed loner with an agenda no one was aware of—a "revolution" against sex and the hippie culture; a revolt against popularity. The young ravers continued with their after-hours party, not knowing that Kyle had a premeditated plan to murder these people, who he felt had contributed to his growing paranoid isolation. One witness said that throughout the entire party, while everyone else was talking, laughing, and having a good time, Kyle just leaned against a wall, silent, looking mad, with his arms crossed over his chest. Then as quietly as he'd entered, he left the party and went down the street to his truck—gathering up, among other things, a Winchester Defender pump-action shotgun and a Ruger P-94 pistol. (Later, officers would find an AR-15, more ammunition, and gas cans full of gasoline still in the bed of his truck.) He also donned two bandoliers completely loaded with shotgun ammunition as well as a pistol holster loaded down with multiple magazines. He meant to kill—there's no question about that.

As Kyle once again approached the residence, he stopped three times to spray-paint the word *Now* on the sidewalk.

Many have theorized about his choice of word, ranging from blaming the Nirvana song "I Want to Know Now" to simply a motivational tool he used to persuade himself to go through with his plan. Regardless, he continued on up the sidewalk with shotgun and pistol in hand. His first victims were two kids on the porch, whom he shot with both guns. He shotgun-blasted another poor soul in the chest who later died from the massive wounds sustained, and who fell back into the house yelling, "I've been shot!" Kyle continued walking over the bodies, trying to push his way inside to continue his killing spree. Others in the house tried to bar him from entering, but one of the victims' legs kept the door from closing, and Huff managed to push his way in. Panic ensued, and kids ran in every direction, many through the kitchen to the back door, while several escaped from windows to the safety of the outside. Others merely hunkered behind couches, hoping and praying not to be seen. Kyle quickly shot five others, killing three, while yelling, "I've got enough ammunition for everyone," as he proceeded to the second floor of the house. At the top of the steps, he blasted two holes into the bathroom while two kids hid in the corner of the hallway. He did not pursue them. As a matter of fact, he didn't pursue anyone else at all, though he really could have killed virtually every last one of them. Instead, Kyle roamed the bedrooms, walked downstairs into the basement, and then exited the dwelling.

By this time, phone calls were rapidly coming in to the police department from residents who had heard the shots being fired. As luck would have it, a patrolman near the house arrived approximately two minutes after the melee began, at nearly the same moment that Kyle came out the front door. One of the injured victims stumbled out of the house as the officer approached, while Kyle came out the opposite side and began walking toward the cop. The officer told him to drop his weapon, but instead without hesitation Kyle opened his mouth, inserted the gun barrel, and blew his own brains out before the officer had even completed his sentence, putting an end to what will forever be known as the Capitol Hill Massacre. In the final tally, six young people ranging in age from fourteen to thirty-two were killed (seven if you count Kyle), and two were seriously wounded.

· · ·

At midafternoon the next day, Mark took us to 2112 East Republican Street—the exact address of the Capitol Hill Massacre. It had been repainted, with new residents now living in the home; it hardly appeared like the scene of the worst crime the city had witnessed in twenty-five years. "What did you think when the call came in?" we asked Mark as we parked conspicuously across the street. The house has become sort of an attraction, a shrine, which people visit on the anniversary of the massacre. "I knew it was going to be an APE," Mark replied, with a fiendish grin. An APE, we learned, is an Acute Political Emergency—code for "Hey, I wanna see a dead body and I want it solved tonight." Crime scenes that are or become

APEs are tough to work because the media wants a story and the department brass want to get into the scene as soon as possible. "I had to keep telling everyone to take a breath," Mark continued. "Telling them it was just like any other crime scene. I hate to sound callous, but you have to look at [the bodies] as evidence; they are not people anymore. The fact that it wasn't a whodunit made everybody calm down a little; otherwise, the stress level would have been even higher." In essence, whether the crime is a simple burglary or a homicide, the system for working a scene is the same. And there is no difference between a homicide with one victim and a high-profile homicide with multiple victims, except that there's more pressure for answers and people want them immediately. But giving in to pressure to work a crime scene faster is when mistakes can be made. Ultimately, the Seattle CSI team worked the scene for two days, rotating shifts so that the scene was always being worked by someone with a fresh set of eyes.

"Was there anything unusual about the case?" we asked Mark as we stared at the old house. Beyond the obvious, of course. "The only thing that came up was that the suspect had a twin brother," Mark replied. This caused a few moments of consternation, considering that the suspect had shot himself in the face, thereby making a visual identification nearly impossible. A homicide supervisor on the scene went into the suspect's wallet to identify him, which is not standard protocol (technically a body is the property of the medical examiner, and no one else is to touch it until the ME has completed the examination).

Seattle Police Department's Crime Scene Unit works the horrific
scene at the Capitol Hill Massacre.
PHOTO TAKEN BY ALAN BERNER, COURTESY THE *SEATTLE TIMES*

"You've got to be flexible at times, and there are exceptions
to every rule," Mark said, regarding the need to obtain Huff's
identification. "We just record what happened in our report so
there are no questions later."

· · ·

After the scene had been worked and the suspect, Kyle Aaron
Huff, had been positively identified through fingerprints, the
case was essentially over from the investigative perspective. But
as with any crime or occurrence, everyone still wanted to know
why. Why did this person commit such a random, violent act?

The Seattle Police Department formed a third-party panel to look into the case and psychologically dissect Kyle's motives to help ease the community's pain. The three-month investigation and analysis of Kyle's behavior concluded that he was a loner with no romantic relationships who liked video games and hard-core music. In an attempt to get inside Huff's psyche, investigators searched his computer and interviewed his relatives and acquaintances. They found that he and his twin brother had both moved to Seattle from Montana, and though he'd tried, Kyle had never seemed to fit in. Based on the panel's investigation, it appeared that Kyle had originally sought out the rave crowd to make friends. But the culture of the ravers, particularly their affinity for being very touchy-feely, may have put him off (Kyle had never had a real romantic relationship with a girl). Many people may have viewed the panel's conclusions as simple guesstimates, based on conjecture, had it not been for another unbelievable event, the last epiphany regarding the Capitol Hill Massacre.

On April 24, 2006, almost exactly one month to the day after the shootings on Capitol Hill, the Seattle bomb squad was called to examine a suspicious-looking package found behind an apartment complex. The landlord of the complex had recently noticed a lot of illegal dumping, so he had been digging around in the Dumpster when he came across a strange-looking object hidden in it. Though the suspicious package turned out to be nothing more than garbage, the landlord had also discovered something nearly as explosive—a suicide letter from Kyle.

Crumpled up in a fast-food bag was a handwritten note

from Kyle addressed to his twin brother, Kane, regarding the events that would unfold on that now infamous day in March. Initially, most people thought the letter was a hoax, especially considering the random circumstances in which it was found. Some have theorized that Kane might have been in possession of the letter and wanted to distance himself. He was known to have passed by that Dumpster several times as he prepared to move out of the Seattle area forever. But how the letter got into the Dumpster remains a mystery. A cursory comparison of the letter to other samples of Kyle's handwriting revealed similarities, but nothing conclusive, so the letter was eventually sent to the Washington State Crime Lab for analysis.

On June 7, the lab released its findings, stating that the letter was in "high probability" written by Kyle Huff. And the contents appeared to be the ravings of a paranoid and troubled young man. The letter was to his brother, ranting about a "revolution" against "a world of sex." Kyle's words wove a delusional tapestry about "killing this hippie shit"—a clear attack on the rave kids whom he ultimately killed in cold blood. Kyle ended the letter with the phrase "Now Kids Now," then signed off by telling Kane that he loved him. Without question, the Capitol Hill Massacre was a tragedy of epic proportions, carried out by a lonely and misguided soul.

• • •

CSIs are real people. Every graduate we spent time with has a family. They are ordinary people, except they have an up-close and inside look at just how crappy the world can truly get. Detective Mark Hanf and his wife are no different. They live in a beautiful condo just outside Seattle. She works for Intel and travels across most of Asia, helping to keep the tech industry booming. They have two adult sons, one who recently came back from the war in Iraq. At dinner, which we ate at a local Mongolian grill, we talked about something other than dead bodies: *American Idol*. It doesn't get much more everyday than that.

The next morning, after a Mongolian buffet hangover, we reconvened with the rest of the crime scene unit down in their office. It's a little macabre, visiting all of these different cities and hoping for crimes to occur, thus giving us crime scenes to work. Yet up to this point, we hadn't had even a sniff of death. But that morning, talk in the department was of a current missing-person case that had caught the attention of the local news media. Flyers had been posted everywhere, and relatives of the missing person had been on television complaining about the police and how little they were doing to find their loved one in the nearly two weeks he'd been missing.

The case was a little strange: On Cinco de Mayo, a father and son had apparently gone down to Pioneer Square to drink, snort cocaine, and, it seems, share a hooker back in their hotel room. (Not our idea of what the holiday's meant for.) There was little information to go on. Supposedly the son had walked out of the bar they'd been drinking at, headed north, and never been heard from since. The father was not considered the most credible witness; he seemed to be sketchy when asked about the events that occurred on the night his son went missing. His timelines did not match the time frames on the bar security camera, and phone calls from the hotel room seemed to contradict his story. Dad said his son had gotten into a fight with the bouncer before he was kicked out of the bar, but the bouncer said something quite different, telling the cops that the father was never even at the bar and that the son had come and gone on his own. Though the father was turning out to look very suspicious, there was nothing warranting an arrest. However, the investigators wanted to talk to him and had scheduled him to be polygraphed the very next day.

The next morning on our way to the department, we stopped at one of our favorite places—Krispy Kreme—and brought in a dozen doughnuts for breakfast, keeping the stereotype alive. (We opted for traditional doughnuts, rather than another Seattle treat—a humbow. A humbow is simply a steamed or baked Asian pastry filled with a very sweet red meat. Think of it as a Krispy Kreme glazed doughnut filled with barbecued pork. Mark had introduced us to them during our first visit to Seattle three years earlier, and we realized that there was another reason for all of the coffee consumption in Seattle—to wake up its residents from humbow-induced comas.) Back in the office, we sat around for a while, doughnuts in hand, talking to Mark about how his NFA training had helped him with his work. "For me, [the most valuable part] was the forensic anthropology component," Mark stated. Not many in his department,

BEHIND THE YELLOW TAPE

with the exception of some members of the Green River Task Force, had ever had any formal training in human remains recovery until then. Just as we were getting deep into the conversation, however, a call out to a crime scene came in.

A body had been discovered underneath the Magnolia Bridge, one of the myriad of bridges permeating the heart of Seattle. They didn't know who it was, what condition the body was in, or even how long it had been there. As a matter of fact, they had no idea if a crime had even taken place. Armed with only this little tidbit of information, we piled into the backseat of an unmarked cruiser with the crime scene van following close behind. The exact location of the body was hard to determine from the initial call. We drove up, down, and all around the Port of Seattle pier trying to find where the body had been discovered. Initially, a security guard working the entrance to the pier barred us entry, even with the flash of a badge. Homeland security is alive and well in Seattle. Finally, after what seemed to be a dizzying quarter of an hour later, we found where we were supposed to go.

The crime scene unit sergeant was already there, awaiting our arrival. And the moment we got out of the car downwind from the body, we could already smell that all-too-familiar smell of human decomposition. As we moved a little closer, we could see the hump of a body lying facedown in the weeds, just a few feet on the other side of a chain-link fence that had been partially torn down.

After gathering what information was available from the

The body of a dead man lies beneath the sheet, having fallen
to his death from the bridge above.
HALLCOX & WELCH, LLC

initial responding officer, the team began to work the scene.
As if they had performed this dance a hundred times before,
they each worked on a different task, never having to speak
but each knowing what the other was doing. Don Ledbetter
(a graduate of Session XIII at the NFA) went to the top of the
bridge to take pictures of the victim, who lay down below. We
assisted Don, directing traffic to keep him from getting run
over. Then Don and Brian Stampfl began mapping the entire
crime scene area with a *total station*, a measuring instrument
used in surveying as well as in crime scene work and traffic

199

collision reconstruction. It is used to electronically measure and map outdoor crime scenes accurately. Lisa Haakenstad (also an NFA alumnus) took notes while Mark assisted wherever necessary. Meanwhile, it had been determined that in all probability, the victim found under the bridge was the same young man who had gone missing twelve days earlier on Cinco de Mayo. Several investigators from both homicide and missing persons were also on the scene trying to confirm that was the case, discovering that a call had come in to 911 on May 5 about a drunken man who'd been seen walking in traffic. The CSIs continued to map, photograph, and work the scene until they reached the body, while the sergeant went to procure the most important tool a Seattle crime scene investigator needs—coffee. Then it was time to call the ME's office.

As the team drank their Starbucks coffee while waiting for the medical examiner to arrive, stress-related black humor began to emerge. Someone started whistling *Ode to Billie Joe*, particularly emphasizing the line that goes "today Billie Joe MacAllister jumped off the Tallahatchie Bridge." Another began referring to May 5 as "Stinko de Mayo." You've got to love the morbid humor of a CSI.

The ME arrived on the scene to a swarm of flies, which had begun hatching right before our eyes. Up until this particular day, the spring weather had been cool and cloudy, with virtually no sun. But on this day the weather was spectacular—too hot for Seattleites—and the warmth had allowed the flies to begin popping from their wiggly cocoons. The victim had been wearing a hooded sweatshirt with the hood pulled up when he'd apparently plunged to his death from the Magnolia Bridge, landing facedown and thus obscuring his face. From all outward appearances, the victim looked "fresh," with no visible signs of decomposition. But when the ME worked his way around to the head area of the victim's body and pulled down the sweatshirt hood, we were privy to the most unnerving sight we had ever experienced.

Pulling off the sweatshirt revealed an approximately eighty- to one-hundred-pound mass of maggots that, once daylight hit them, vanished within seconds, down into the thoracic cavity of the victim. Amazingly, from the bottom of his neck to the top of his head, the victim was completely gnawed down to the bone, while the rest of his body looked essentially whole and not decomposed. The spine had been severed from the trauma of the fall, and the only thing that was holding the victim's head in place was the sweatshirt hood. Flies lay eggs only in moist places, which typically, not counting wounds, are the eyes, ears, nose, mouth, and genitals. But a fully clothed man, with a hood on, lying facedown, doesn't provide much access for the flies. However, the fall had clearly broken the man's neck violently, thus leaving a wet and warm wound for the flies to infiltrate and begin their habitation of the victim's corpse. The medical examiner had never seen anything like it. Nor had we.

The maggot mass had taken on a life of its own, and even later in the cooler at the morgue, they continued to eat away at the victim—from the inside out. The ME, with help from the CSIs, removed the body from under the bridge, placed it on a board, and loaded it into the truck. The scene had been worked, and the case had essentially been solved. A drunk guy had fallen off a bridge. After the body was removed, we left to go back to the processing area to wash the decomp off our shoes and get ready to visit with another of our favorite NFA graduates in Seattle.

Detective Tim Devore (a graduate of Session X) was the second person from Seattle to ever grace our doorstep in Knoxville. Tim is the Dean Martin of CSIs; if it had been election year in Knoxville during his session, he would easily have been elected mayor. Tim simply has the type of personality that

Seattle Police Department, Washington, personnel: Mark Hanf, Brian Stampfl, Lisa Haakenstad, and Don Ledbetter.

HALLCOX & WELCH, LLC

everyone gravitates toward. He had been an alternate with the CSI unit when he came through the program, and ultimately chose to work full time in the homicide unit. We met him and his partner for dinner. Tim had picked a great restaurant right on the water, Maggie Bluff's—which, as luck would have it, turned out to be about a hundred feet from where we had spent all day collecting the remains of the fellow who'd fallen from the bridge.

"How's homicide?" we asked Tim. "I'm the fifth wheel," he replied, flicking his sport coat open. Tim is one of the few cops in the Seattle Police Department who still dresses like the stereotypical detective, minus the tie, regardless of the relaxed dress code. His fellow detective, Jeff Mudd, who happens to be related to the doctor who patched up John Wilkes Booth after he had assassinated President Lincoln, looked as if he were dressed for fly fishing. Being the fifth wheel in the homicide unit essentially means you're the paper pusher, taking overflow from the others who are already established and working felony assaults. Tim's current assignment also includes being on a task force that is going through some of the 296 cases that had been overturned on a technicality by the courts back in 2004. Of particular interest to Tim, as well as the rest of his department, was the possibility of an overturned conviction of a man who had murdered one of their comrades, Detective Antonio Terry.

"I've interviewed over sixty convicted thugs across the state," Detective Devore said, regarding the Terry case. "It took me a while to understand the prison lingo. I'd start off each interview with, 'How long have you been here?' and I'd get an answer like, 'A minute.' I finally found out that 'a minute' was any time less than six months." Tim talked about how he had interviewed members of the Black Gangster Disciples, trying to develop leads on whether the person convicted for killing Detective Terry had ever talked about killing a cop. Most just clammed up when asked if they knew anything, but one finally talked. They would use him to try to keep the cop killer in prison for good.

"I'd just said bye to Antonio," Tim continued somberly. He began to quietly tell us about Antonio, how good he was as an undercover at buying dope and how he'd put on liquid glove (a chemical skin protectant) to protect his hands from the ass-ridden dope he would buy. (On the street many dealers hide their goods in their rectum, so if they are searched it won't be easily found.) He talked about how Antonio had joked with him and the other guys about his wife's reaction to the smell of his hands, and how he'd said good-bye to them as he headed for the South Precinct. Devore talked about how great a guy Detective Terry was, and how he had stopped on his way to help two thugs whose car had broken down, but when he'd pulled over to help, one had yelled, "He's a cop!" and a gun battle had ensued. Tim told us that Antonio had shot one of the suspects and had been shot himself, yet had still managed to drive back to the precinct, staggering in and yelling "I'm shot!" Tim continued on, getting quieter, telling us how the bullet had ratcheted through the artery in Antonio's hip, how they pumped blood into him for two hours and how it flowed out, and how he had heart attack after heart attack after heart attack, and finally died from a massive coronary. "We all heard he'd been shot in the stomach and were relieved," Tim said, having hardly touched his food. "Your chances are good with those types of gunshots." But it was not to be, and Detective Antonio Terry was senselessly killed, leaving behind a wife and a young child. Tim has made it his mission to see that the perp who murdered his friend doesn't get out of prison on an overturned technicality.

We talked for hours about crime scenes, the training, and how we all had come to know one another. As we got up from the table to leave, Detective Devore, in typical chamber of commerce fashion, decided to take us to the top of one of the hills surrounding Seattle, the perfect spot to see the wonderful skyline at night. We commemorated our last night in Seattle with a picture of the view. Exhausted and with the smell of decomp still stuck in our nostrils, we went back to our rooms to get some sleep for our long journey home.

The next morning, as we prepared to leave Seattle, we received a call from CSI Detective Mark Hanf. "We've got a homicide," he said excitedly. Go figure. It's impossible to predict when crime is going to occur. Crime analysts are employed by virtually every police department in the country to provide statistical analysis on crimes and crime trends. But those are still only trends and best guesstimates. No one ever knows when the drunk guy will get mad enough to stab another drunk

The authors with Mark Hanf and Detective Tim Devore in Seattle.
HALLCOX & WELCH, LLC

over a game of pool, or when an angry wife will shoot her husband as he comes in from work.

Violence has no true identity and no true probability, which is a scary proposition for those in charge of figuring out who done it. But with CSIs like Mark around, we feel confident that he and his team will figure out who did it, all with an over-caffeinated grin and a *venti* cup tossed somewhere in the background.

7

Jersey Devil

UNION COUNTY SHERIFF'S OFFICE, NEW JERSEY

UNION COUNTY

NEW JERSEY

Union County, New Jersey, was founded in 1857 and is considered part of the greater New York metropolitan area. Elizabeth, the county seat, is the fourth-largest city in New Jersey, helping to make Union County one of the densest counties in the nation. Elizabeth was the first capital of New Jersey, but it is usually overshadowed by its bigger sister Newark to the north. The sheriff's office employs 215 people. Thirty-seven murders occurred in the county in 2006.

New Jersey is famous for a lot of things. Thomas Edison, the Atlantic City Boardwalk, *The Sopranos*; even the first baseball game ever played was in New Jersey. But something that is less known about New Jersey is that it's full of ghosts. That's right, ghosts. Ghosts, ghouls, goblins, and creatures of every kind. Some say that New Jersey is the most haunted state in the union, and many famous apparitions call it home, including the ghosts of Captain Kidd's pirate crew, Joseph Bonaparte (Napoleon's younger brother), and the celebrated Jersey Devil, a wicked winged and hoofed creature that sprung straight from its mother's womb. It still wreaks havoc today in the fields, farms, and streams along the Jersey shore.

We came face-to-face with a Jersey Devil in Knoxville, Tennessee, on a warm Sunday evening in early May 2005. This devil was a female, dressed in all black, with long jet-black hair and nails, accompanied by her giant of a husband, who had very short buzzed, brownish-blond hair and a walk reminiscent of Karl from *Sling Blade*. All that was missing was some goat's blood and for someone to ask for "biscuits and mustard, hmm." Just as we began the introductions to begin Session XII, the devil's phone went off, blaring the theme music from *The Godfather*. With that auspicious beginning, we knew we were in for quite an experience. She scared us a little, and we think we scared her too. Her name is Melissa DeFilippo.

Melissa is the sergeant of the crime scene unit for the sheriff's office in Union County, New Jersey. Union County is composed of twenty-one different municipalities, including the city of Elizabeth (home to none other than *The Sopranos*). As a matter of fact, you can take a *Sopranos* tour, similar to Kramer's "The Real J. Peterman Tour" from *Seinfeld*, visiting such world-renowned landmarks as the spot where Big Pussy talked to the FBI. The heavy Italian influence on the area is self-evident, and in fact Melissa, Frankie Coon, and Adrian Furman (all graduates of the program and all Union County CSIs) all have thick jet-black hair and look like they could be the bastard children of Tony Soprano himself. (Though our most recent graduate from Union County, Lauren Guenther, is a redhead, so go figure.)

Union County is a very *blue* county, with the longest-standing sheriff, Sheriff Ralph Froehlich, in the entire United States. His fifty-plus years dedicated to law enforcement is an incredible achievement. And he is living proof that progressiveness and youth are not necessarily correlated. Melissa contacted our office and was able to come through the program on a scholarship reserved for the first person to represent a state. "We'll never send anybody else because of cost," Melissa told us early on during her session. But now Union County has had a total of six graduates of the program, and all but Melissa paid the full tuition. And the sheriff can take full credit for having the vision to make his department better. His department's successes have put his CSIs in charge of all murders and officer-involved shootings for all of the municipalities that reside within the county of Union. This decree was put out by the prosecutor's office, which saw firsthand the knowledge gained by graduates processing crime scenes in New Jersey.

Melissa had it tough in the beginning of the program, and we certainly didn't do her any favors. Each student gets randomly teamed up with another tablemate for ten weeks, to work together and support each other. Her tablemate was Mark Turner, the detective from Sevier County, Tennessee. Imagine for a moment what Larry the Cable Guy might sound like trying to talk with his nose stuffed full of cotton and his mouth filled with molasses. That's Mark. Then imagine this cotton-and-molasses-filled Larry trying to communicate with a gal whose Jersey accent is as thick as the cream in a cannoli. It was like a screwed-up United Nations meeting without a translator. Shoulder shrugs and turned-down mouths were the only modes of communication for the first several days. In Melissa's defense, even we Knoxvillians had trouble understanding Mark's incredible southern drawl.

Melissa admitted that on day one, she was in tears calling home, telling her husband, Mike, who had gone back to New Jersey, that she already wanted to come home. But by day three, she was in the bathroom on the phone to her boss, saying, "Hey, I get it, we learn by tawking"—though to this day, she still has problems with many southern colloquialisms, particularly the phrase, "jam up and jelly tight." But by week five, she had become the unofficial mother hen of the group, making Italian dishes for the whole class at night and cooking a traditional New Jersey breakfast dish, lovingly referred to as a "Jersey Breakfast," for all of us one morning. Melissa fried up slices of Taylor ham and coupled them with eggs, cheese, salt, pepper, and ketchup to create a wonderful breakfast sandwich. She actually flew home just to get the ham and brought it back in her carry-on luggage. Sergeant DeFilippo made such an impression on everyone that in the end, she won the coveted Dr. Bass Excellence in Forensic Science Award, proving that bad girls can be good.

We visited Melissa and Mike at their home in New Jersey on a cold day in early December 2006. Christmas lights had sprung up around the neighborhood, shaking off the cobwebs of northeastern basements and attics everywhere. Christmas seems to begin earlier up north because of the cold temperatures, which tempers crime just a bit. Melissa ran to the door, greeting us with her usual hugs and kisses, and Mike, with his typical Archie Bunker/Jerry Lewis voice and his pet parrot on his shoulder, gave us both a kiss on each cheek, something we came to love about New Jersey. Mike is quite the jokester and a hell of a storyteller. After ordering a typical New Jersey–Italian meal of pizza, Mike jumped right into some of his war stories.

"Hey, youse guys ever hear of the bunny test?" Mike asked. Neither of us had. The bunny test is an apocryphal story made famous in New York, though everyone denies ever having heard of it. Plausible deniability is every policeman's motto. The bunny test begins simply enough when an investigator starts interrogating a suspect. If the investigator gets nowhere, he gets up and leaves the room, without ever saying a word. Fifteen minutes pass, which is enough time to make the suspect begin to wonder what's going on. And that's when it happens. The door bursts open, and in comes a guy dressed head to toe in a pink bunny suit, with an orange billy club made to look like a giant carrot. He continues with the interrogation, but unlike the investigator, with the first sign of resistance, he proceeds to beat the shit out of the guy with the carrot until he tells the bunny what he wants to hear. Then he gets up, flops his ears back, and leaves. Another fifteen minutes pass, and the original investigator comes back, acting oblivious as to what the suspect is claiming to have happened. In court, when the suspect tells the story of being beaten by a pink rabbit, the judge disregards it as the rantings of a madman. That is, until many suspects begin to complain about the "wascawy wabbit." Needless to say, the bunny test is now frowned on. Too bad.

There are many similar stories around the country about

how police officers get confessions in strange, but less violent ways. For instance, many an investigator has gotten a confession from none other than a copy machine. They just tell the suspect that the machine can tell if he or she is lying or telling the truth. Then, after the investigator's question, and depending on the desired answer, he or she puts a piece of paper into the machine, which copies the word *yes* or *no*, spitting it out into the tray in front of the suspect, confirming the answer and proving him or her to be a liar. Some even go a step further and hook a suspect to the department's AED (automated external defibrillator), telling the poor ignorant soul that it is a lie detector. Thank God for dumb criminals.

After Mike was finished with his police stories, we talked a little bit about the week ahead. Sunday, the day we arrived, was the start of Melissa's on-call shift, when she could be called out to any scene that happened—day or night. We had come prepared with warm clothes just in case that happened. The year 2006 had been pretty busy for Union County, which typically gets between forty and fifty homicides per year. Compared to Knoxville, Tennessee, which gets about ten to fifteen, and Duluth, Minnesota, which gets somewhere in the single-digit range, the number seems pretty significant. So, as we had in other cities, we were macabrely hoping to see a good crime scene. And indeed, after about our second piece of pizza, Melissa's pager went off. *Bingo*, we thought as we scurried around for our gloves and hats. But we hadn't been paying attention to Mike, who had grabbed the phone and gone into the other room to make a crank call. Good ol' Mike. We left the DeFilippos' with our bellies full of pizza, hoping beyond hope that the Jersey thugs would wait at least one more night so we could get some sleep.

With a peaceful night behind us, we started the next morning by sitting down with Sheriff Ralph Froehlich at his office. Sheriff Froehlich is a consummate professional, welcoming us with open arms and applauding us for our contributions to the world of law enforcement. He's also a consummate politician, never failing to miss an opportunity for a news story or a photo opportunity, and he had us pose along with the other graduates of our program out in the front lobby. Well, it was an election year after all.

The authors with Union County Sheriff's Office, New Jersey, personnel: Frank Coon, Melissa DeFilippo, and Adrian Furman.
COURTESY OF THE UNION COUNTY SHERIFF'S OFFICE, NEW JERSEY

BEHIND THE YELLOW TAPE

The sheriff has certainly seen a lot during his long tenure in office. But for him, one of the best compliments that had ever been paid to him or to his department was when the Union County prosecutor's office determined that because of the skills of his CSI Unit, they would be in charge of all homicides across the twenty-one municipalities—a true testament to their success. "Most chiefs come up and almost kiss me, grateful for the work we do," Sheriff Froehlich told us from behind his large desk adorned with more than half a century's worth of law enforcement accoutrements. "Hell, I shoulda been dead years ago," he told us later, because of an illness that was supposed to be fatal. "Even an old dog can learn new tricks." Admittedly, many departments with older chiefs or sheriffs are reluctant to try new things, being happy and content with the status quo—that is also to say, happy and somewhat lazy. Not every chief within the county wants to kiss the sheriff. After all, murders are a lot of work. A suicide, not so much. And when there is doubt, politics can come into play.

"Wanna see a mummy?" Melissa asked us as we were released back into her custody. Finding a mummy at a crime scene is a rarity and elicits excitement, being the Holy Grail of forensic evidence. "He's a Juan Doe," Melissa told us as she gathered up the crime scene photos, *Juan* referring to the unknown person being of Hispanic ethnicity. "How was the body found?" we asked, looking through the disgusting crime scene pictures. "Bad smell," she replied, with an upturned nose. It's certainly amazing how many bodies are discovered by smell, with neighbors invariably saying, "Well, I hadn't seen him in a while and now that you mention it, I had been smelling something funny." In this case, construction workers called in to do a renovation on a house had called the police after stumbling into the bad smell, and Union County CSIs were dispatched to the scene when police found the dead body. The police had concluded within minutes that the deceased had committed suicide, strangling himself with an electrical cord, but they hadn't given the crime scene more than a cursory look.

Sergeant Frankie Coon was the first CSI to the scene. Frankie is the brooding guy of the group. The police told him right away that it was a suicide, but, not convinced, he decided to take a look for himself. "Frankie called me within a few minutes," Melissa began as we made our way out to the crime scene van. "He thought it was a possible homicide, so I went to the scene to help him out." Once the New Jersey CSIs took over, the police on scene essentially stepped out.

"When I got to the scene, it was obvious to me that it was a homicide," Melissa said as we drove into the city of Elizabeth. "There were pools of old, dried blood, with fine spatter above the body," she explained. "The victim's pants pockets were turned inside out, and a large container of rat poison was placed at his head. There were also many footwear impressions left in blood, but the victim was barefoot. Even if the prints were from his shoes, someone had removed them—they were nowhere to be found." She added, "If it was a suicide, it was unlike any suicide I'd ever heard of or seen."

At the autopsy of Juan Doe, a strange circumstance was unveiled. Not only was an electrical cord wrapped around his neck, but there was also a dress, and underneath the dress was a coat hanger. Three different objects had been used to strangle this poor guy to death. Yet the medical examiner corroborated the police's determination and listed suicide as the manner of death.

Frustrated, Melissa and Frankie continued on with what they could with regard to the case. Pieces from the man's femur have been sent to the University of North Texas for DNA extraction in an effort to enter Juan into the missing person's database. The blood was also swabbed and collected to see if it might have belonged to someone other than just Juan. The severity of its degradation has made this comparison difficult. Unfortunately, this may be the only way to ever establish the possibility of the case being a homicide. "What do you think happened?" we asked, walking down the street in Elizabeth, down near the shores of the Arthur Kell River, where they filmed the opening to *The Sopranos*, feeling sort of like the Beatles walking down Abbey Road. "It's probably a gang murder or a gang initiation," Melissa said. "Frankie thinks the rat poison and the turned-out pockets are references to the victim being a rat." Regardless of who or why or even how, the main focus is just to identify the victim—which seems to be a long shot at best. Juan was probably an illegal alien, which makes the possibility of discovering who he was that much harder.

The number of missing people is growing exponentially

every year. The federal government's best estimate of the number of missing and unidentified persons in the United States is roughly five thousand. But those in the know, the people who work in this arena every day, estimate that number to be roughly ten times that—a staggering fifty thousand missing and unidentified persons, many of whom will never be identified no matter what the advances in forensic science or how much evidence comes to light. Reasons for this vary, but the practice of most medical examiners' offices, particularly ten to twenty years ago, was to simply get rid of unclaimed bodies through either cremation or burial in potter's fields—with little to no identifiable markings. Hopefully, if DNA can be extracted from Juan's femur, he may be identified and returned to his loved ones. But more than likely, Juan Doe will be added to that ever-growing list of "never to be knowns."

On our second night in Union County, Sheriff Froehlich invited us and the CSI Unit out for a nice dinner. Melissa made reservations at a wonderfully fancy Italian restaurant, Ristorante da Benito, which often boasts major players in New Jersey politics. On this night, ex–New Jersey governor James McGreevey was having dinner with other politicians from the area. The DeFilippo name carries significant weight in Union; Melissa's mother-in-law is the Democratic chair for the county. And Melissa herself is obviously known among the political elite, as we saw when McGreevey came over to give her a kiss on the cheek.

The sheriff sat at the head of the table, talking about the

"olden days" as we dipped crunchy Italian breads into olive oil seasoned with herbs. "In my day," the sheriff began, leaning back a bit in his chair, "the CSI was the mayor's detective, [someone who] was appointed by him. And he probably was a nephew or a cousin or whatever," the sheriff theorized. "He carried a box camera, a magnifying glass, a little dusting brush, and would just dust every damn thing he would come up to, never finding anything."

"But," he conceded, "that was crime scene work back then."

Sheriff Froehlich carries himself in a dignified and confident manner, yet is somehow still grandfatherly. The sheriff has lived a long time and has spent more than a half a century dealing with every facet of law enforcement. "In all my years, a lot of changes have taken place and they have taken a long time, but in five years you guys have done more in one subject, in one area, than I have seen in my fifty years in all of law enforcement," he said. "Look at where you guys are today; holy smoke!" And with that superb speech and ringing endorsement, dinner was served.

The next morning, we began our quest again in search of crime. After all, New Jersey is certainly well known for its crime. Camden is one of the most dangerous cities in the United States; Jimmy Hoffa is probably buried under concrete somewhere in the Garden State if he wasn't ground up and made into hot dogs. Whereas most people kill people with simple things like guns, knives, bare hands, or broken bottles, New

Jerseyans have been known to raise the bar. Like using a bike,
for instance. Melissa had a recent homicide case where the victim had been killed with a bicycle. He wasn't beaten to death
with the handlebars or strangled to death with the chain or
even bludgeoned with the kickstand. No, the guy was beaten
to death with the whole friggin' bike. Now that's dedication,
when you can kill someone with a Schwinn.

"What's the worst crime scene you've been a part of?" we
asked Melissa as we drove around some of the more affluent
areas in Union County with her partner, a Beastie Boys wannabe who kept saying, "Here come the po-po."

"We had a domestic on Super Bowl Sunday in 2005,"
Melissa began, slapping her partner to shut him up. It's an
urban legend that up to 40 percent more domestic violence cases
occur on Super Bowl Sunday in the United States compared to
any other day because of the disproportionate amount of sore-
losing bettors. But Melissa's case, though it was a domestic,
had nothing to do with football, and everything to do with a
sick and very troubled mother.

• • •

New Jersey State Troopers discovered Lynn Giovanni
crashed into a guardrail along Route 78 in Roselle, New Jersey. "Roselle's a pretty nice area," Melissa said as we continued driving. Simply put, "nice areas," whether in New Jersey
or Arkansas, are less likely to have homicides. It's just a fact.
And almost invariably, when CSIs are dispatched to cases in

these areas, it's for crimes of familiarity, not ones of random violence.

Lynn was taken to the hospital and treated for minor wounds. She then dropped a bomb on the unsuspecting troopers, telling them rather nonchalantly that she had murdered her daughter, Nicole, and had been trying to kill herself by crashing her car (though some disbelieve her tale about the attempted suicide, considering how minor the actual crash was). Troopers were dispatched to Lynn's house and had to bust down the door to get in. That's where they found the unthinkable.

"She was a very popular, all-American girl," Melissa said of Nicole Giovanni, the fourteen-year-old girl who had been brutally beaten by her mother while she slept. Lynn Giovanni had beaten her daughter from behind with a hammer, many times. But as Lynn would admit later in court, "she kept breathing." Lynn then turned to a shovel, but "it was too hard to swing," and again, "she kept breathing." So Lynn returned to using the hammer to finally kill Nicole.

"Adrian, she was the first CSI to the scene," Melissa said. Officer Adrian Furman is the pretty, straight-talking, artistic one of the group. Adrian has a knack for working on some of the more gruesome cases. She worked the macabre and eerie scene, jumping each time the radiator in the bedroom clicked on and off, as Nicole lay there motionless and covered in blood. "We're just not used to normal-looking people at scenes," Melissa admitted. Most crimes, the ones that don't end up as national news, are committed by people who are "high risk," like drug dealers, prostitutes, and meth heads. Cases like those of Natalee Holloway and JonBenét Ramsey, though well known and highly publicized, are not the norm. They are aberrations in the crime statistics. "Nicole's room looked like my room when I was a teenager, except all of her posters and teddy bears were spattered with blood. Sad," Melissa said.

"I didn't respond to the initial call; I was sent there to do the blood reconstruction in case the mother decided to change her story later," Melissa continued. "Nicole was gone, but all of the blood evidence was still there." At the time of Lynn's confession and subsequent arrest, no one was sure that she would stick to her story. The Union County CSIs wanted to make sure that the evidence in the room corroborated the mother's

The home of Nicole Giovanni—Roselle Park, New Jersey.
COURTESY OF THE UNION COUNTY SHERIFF'S OFFICE, NEW JERSEY

original confession. Melissa's job was to string the blood scene and calculate the area of origin for Nicole's head when she had been struck. She performed the calculations at the scene and mathematically reconstructed the events, placing the area of origin about eight inches above the bed—precisely where Nicole's head would have been on her pillow. "It was amazing, seeing that stuff work," Melissa enthused about bloodstain pattern analysis.

In the end, the mother stuck to her story and was able to plead down to aggravated manslaughter—a sentence of thirty years, of which she must serve twenty-five and a half. Lynn had been sent to a psychiatric hospital, forgoing bail, and had been diagnosed with bipolar disorder during her medical incarceration, a condition probably made worse by her recent divorce. This was significant in allowing her to be able to plead down her crime to manslaughter. New Jersey law stipulates that before a person can be charged with a murder, the state must prove two things beyond a reasonable doubt: First, the person must have caused the victim's death or serious bodily injury that then results in death—of which Lynn clearly was guilty. Then, if the first criterion is met, the state must prove beyond a reasonable doubt that the defendant did so purposely or knowingly. New Jersey prosecutors, knowing that Lynn had been diagnosed as being bipolar, didn't believe that they could prove that she "knowingly" killed Nicole. Thus, they allowed the plea of aggravated manslaughter to be entered. Lynne's ex-husband, Nicole's father, sat in the courtroom as the verdict came down, and he was quoted as saying to Lynn, "I hope you and your soul rot and burn in hell for eternity." He had hoped for her to receive a much stronger sentence, vying for the death penalty.

Nicole was the second teen from the Roselle area to have been brutally killed within the previous few months. The other young girl, Judy Cajuste, age fourteen, had been found in a Newark Dumpster after being reported missing. Judy is believed to have been a victim of cyberstalking. To date, no arrests have been made in her case. Public outcry over these two murders compelled New Jersey assemblyman Neil Cohen to introduce a bill dubbed "Judy and Nikki's Law" that would provide a mandatory life sentence without parole for anyone who murders a young person under age sixteen. The bill unanimously passed the assembly in 2006, and in 2007 the Senate received it. To date, it is still awaiting review by the Senate Judiciary Committee.

"We actually had another domestic in an even more upscale area almost exactly one year later," Melissa said. "I was on call on New Year's Day in 2006 when the call came in from Cranford, New Jersey. I had bronchitis really bad, and I was thinking, 'What's going on in Cranford? There's no crime.'"

Indeed, Cranford has remarkably little violent crime, years passing without a single homicide. But 2006 was ushered in with a tragic turn of events, the first murder since 2001. "It was a nice house that still had its Christmas wreath on the door," Melissa recalls, of Mary Ellen Touris's house on Retford Avenue in Cranford. Inside the house was a different story. "There were Christmas bulbs smashed, a footstool through the wall, and the owner of the home was found at the bottom of the basement stairs. And the boyfriend was nowhere to be found."

Mary Ellen had been savagely beaten, with huge bruises all over her body. A large one on her neck was in the pattern of a shoe—the same shoe print that was found in dust in the dining room. "I could tell that she had run all over the house, trying to avoid whoever had eventually killed her," Melissa said, of the crime scene. "There was a clump of hair found on the second floor, and blood swipes leading down the stairs. And the soles of her feet were as black as coal where she had continued to run around in the basement."

The home of Mary Ellen Touris—Cranford, New Jersey.
COURTESY OF THE UNION COUNTY SHERIFF'S OFFICE, NEW JERSEY

Detectives searched the entire county for the boyfriend, Christopher Pessolano, who had ironically been stopped earlier that day for driving erratically, but let go. He was finally tracked down in a hotel room, with a pile of bloody clothes stashed in the corner. They found his car also, with blood smeared in it. Though Pessolano immediately claimed that the blood was not Mary Ellen's, the lab determined that it was. "Were there any other pieces of evidence that tied Pessolano to the crime?" we asked, as we exited the car back at the department. "No, he lived there, so his shoe prints, DNA, and fingerprints would be there," Melissa responded. "It was the blood evidence found elsewhere that tied him back to the crime." Pessolano ultimately pleaded guilty and was charged with first-degree murder and sentenced to twenty-five years in prison.

. . .

"We're in charge of fingerprinting and fingerprints," Melissa said to us the next morning, our last day in Union County. We walked outside and under the jail to where the fingerprinting is conducted. Sheriff's offices across the United States are traditionally in charge of fingerprinting people who have been arrested and booking prisoners into incarceration. In Union County, the crime scene unit is in charge of fingerprinting everybody who was committed to jail the night before. They are also, unfortunately, in charge of taking the DNA swabs. "Who gets swabbed?" we asked Sergeant DeFilippo as Frankie struggled to roll one arrestee's fingerprints properly.

"Everybody convicted of an indictable offense," she answered, eyeing Frankie's growing frustration. Little known to all those wannabe CSIs are some of the more menial tasks involved, such as trying to get a good set of prints while wrestling drunks and others not too happy with the po-pos. But even worse than that is the swabbing. People with bleeding gums or those who haven't bathed since God knows when aren't too helpful about having the inside of their mouths swabbed with a giant cotton swab. Some lick it, some bite it, and some even swallow it. Other glamorous duties of the CSI include pubic hair combing; fingernail and toenail scraping; penile, vaginal, and anal swabs; and collecting vomit and fecal matter. Ah yes, the real life of a crime scene investigator that television never shows.

After watching the printing and the swabbing, we walked back to the department to process some evidence. Since graduating from the program, Union County CSIs have become locally known gurus in crime scene processing. Surrounding jurisdictions sometimes get Melissa and her guys to process evidence from their cases. Many things have changed in the unit since Melissa returned from her training, from large things like replacing 35-mm film cameras with digital cameras to small things like the way they dress, moving to the more appropriate BDU (battle dress uniform). The BDU is the typical uniform worn by crime scene investigators as well as other law enforcement officers. This rugged uniform gets its name from the standard-issue uniform that the U.S. military wore in combat.

They also commandeered a supply closet and turned it into

a processing lab, just big enough for a couple of superglue-fuming hoods. An officer had given them a piece of a plastic bag from the scene of a robbery. "We'll try it," DeFilippo said. It takes about twelve to fifteen minutes for quick superglue-fuming to find fingerprints on an item; alas, after fifteen minutes, no prints appeared. "It's like that sometimes," she said, with resignation.

We then moved over to Adrian, who was preparing to appear in court and making a very large representation of an arrested suspect's fingerprints. One side of the posterboard had an enlarged version of the actual print, and the other side showed the comparison print from the scene, with minutiae highlighted to show the identifying characteristics that made

Melissa DeFilippo and her partner looking at the results of superglue-fuming on a piece of evidence.
HALLCOX & WELCH, LLC

the fingerprint unique. "Adrian, have you used any technique from the training at a scene recently?" we asked her as she stared intently at her fingerprint posters. "Yeah, I had this one case where I used Bluestar in a bathroom and the sink lit up like a Christmas tree," she responded gleefully. Bluestar is one of the chemical products that we were first introduced to by one of our students at the academy. Bluestar is essentially luminol on steroids. Both products are latent blood reagents that react to the trace proteins found in blood. They are both particularly useful when trying to detect trace amounts of blood left behind after cleanup with a cleaning agent such as bleach. Both sparkle like fireworks in reaction with bleach, but the places that continue to stay lit, so to speak, is where the blood evidence is. Unlike luminol, which must be used in complete darkness, Bluestar can be used where there is a fair amount of light. Not only that, but Bluestar simply reacts stronger and longer to trace amounts of blood evidence. Bluestar is fast becoming the new standard in blood detection.

Melissa, Adrian, Frankie, and the other CSIs had been introduced to Bluestar at the academy, but the case Adrian mentioned had been her first opportunity to use it on a real case. The suspect in the case was trying to cover up everything. It turned out to be a sexual homicide, but there was very little blood evidence. The suspect said that as he was "doing her," the victim's breathing got slower and slower, and he claimed that she'd basically perished while in the throes of passion. He also said there wasn't much blood, but he had certainly cleaned

Adrian Furman working on her fingerprint chart for court.
HALLCOX & WELCH, LLC

up his mess, washing his hands, towels, and other objects in and around the bathroom. That's where Adrian used the Blue-star to prove that the suspect had been calculated in his actions and in fact had cleaned up a lot of blood, a hell of a lot of blood. "He even changed her shirt after she died," Adrian noted. Ironically, and no one knows if it was on purpose, the shirt he put on his victim had the sentence "God has treated me well" printed across the front of it in large purple letters. "There wasn't a whole lot of blood at the scene, but the bath-room sink really lit up. People are stupid; they can't ever clean up enough."

We then moved back into the video room with Melissa to ask her a few last questions before we broke for the night, so we could finish the evening with a home cooked meal at the DeFilippos' house before we departed to head back to Tennessee.

"Is there a case that eats at you?" we asked Sergeant DeFilippo, as we had every other CSI we visited with on our road adventure.

"There was one recently; it hasn't gone to trial, but it was sad," Melissa replied. The word *sad* really seems to define her, especially when discussing her cases.

. . .

"There was a 911 call from Perth Amboy, from a cell phone," Melissa continued, "but it bounced off a tower in New York City. The 911 operator dispatched officers to places that sounded like what the woman was saying, but they of course never found her." Two days later, the woman was found dead, dumped in a large bag by the side of the road.

Investigators discovered that the victim had been on an interview for a potential nanny job with the man who was now a suspect. He worked as an auto-body technician, and coincidentally the bag the woman's body was found in was very similar to ones used at the shop where the suspect worked. Tiny beads typically used in sandblasting were also found both in the bag and in the suspect's car. Though the beads could not be specifically placed to any one locale, the bag was determined to have come from the shop where the suspect worked. Investigators continued to process the auto-body bay but found nothing.

At the suspect's house, very little evidence was found either. But one of the detectives did find a cell phone in a bathroom drawer, and the last call registered on the phone was to 911. "Apparently, she had gone to the bathroom and made a call with a cell phone she had found in the house," Melissa said, about the poor young woman. "Once they got the call, they could hear her being yelled at to get out of the bathroom." The victim probably thought she'd be saved, desperately waiting for the police to come, but no one ever showed. Because the cell had hit on a New York City tower, the 911 call was dispatched to New York City officers, never realizing that the call was coming from across the river in New Jersey. If the call had bounced off another tower, her fate might have been different.

. . .

"There wasn't much evidence," Melissa said, of the crime scene. However, "there was something weird though when they found the body; she had maggots on her chest, but no wound."

"There shouldn't be maggots there," we responded to Melissa, trying to figure out reasons why there would be. Typically, flies lay eggs only in the moist, warm areas of a victim, such as the nostrils, ears, eyes, anus, and pubic area. But if there is an open wound, such as a slit throat or a gunshot wound, then maggots will lay eggs in those areas as well.

"Well, and it probably won't make it into court, but investigators worked out some street information on the guy, and supposedly, he liked to have sex with prostitutes and finish on their chests," Melissa explained.

"That'd probably do it," we replied, a little dazed, never having thought about flies laying their eggs in sperm. The case is still pending trial.

Our experience in Union County, New Jersey, was a little surprising. As the crow flies, the county is only twelve miles from New York City, and yet it has a relatively low crime rate. On average, the CSI unit works roughly forty homicides per year—just over three per month and just under one per week. (There were none during the four days that we spent in Union County. Perhaps we're good-luck charms.) But whether you're talking about Gary, Indiana, or Beverly Hills, California, every city or county in the United States has crime related to three elements—drugs, sex, and money. Without those things, crime would be nonexistent.

With our interviews, ride-alongs, and penal swabs finished, we headed to the DeFilippos' house for another dinner with the CSI unit—an Italian Last Supper, if you will. Most of the crime scene investigators were in attendance for the prosciutto and melon, the made-from-scratch dishes doused in red and white sauces, and the sopping up of the juices with fresh Italian bread. Frankie, fashionably late as usual, brought a bounty of fresh cannolis from an old-school Italian bakery that has been in Elizabeth since the Statue of Liberty arrived in the harbor. The conversation around the table started out typical for cops, telling the bad things, the funny things, the gross things, and the things not for public consumption. And after some good Italian wine, some ghost stories were told.

"Youse guys know we used to live in a haunted house?" Mike asked the group.

Silence fell on the group for a second, until Frankie said, "Getthefuckouttahere!"

"It's true," Mike insisted, over the laughter, breaking off a piece of bread. Mike then proceeded to tell some elaborate ghost stories about how one of Melissa's Looney Tunes figurines, Gossamer to be exact, would mysteriously find its way from its shelf on the bathroom wall down to the commode lid. It would be sitting there staring at them when they returned home for the evening. Mike told how his Xbox video game system, which he kept on a TV tray in the living room, would be found overturned and stacked under the tray when he got up the next morning. And he told stories of 911 calls that came from inside the home when nobody was there. Most of the group continued to laugh, skeptical of ghosts and Mike's stories. Then Mike and Melissa told a whopper.

"A friend of ours and her kid came up one time," Melissa began as we huddled around listening like we were kids at

BEHIND THE YELLOW TAPE

summer camp. "We were just sitting around talking and her little boy looked up at the stairs and said, 'Who is the funny-looking man?' At the same time, the dog began to growl at empty space." Hair stood up on the backs of our necks. The Jersey Devil lives!

After a few more stories and a few more cannolis, it was time for us to go. The New Jersey CSIs are our dear friends, and we stood in the threshold of the doorway for an eternity, cheek-kissing everyone, Melissa never wanting us to go and us never wanting to leave. It was the custom back in the old days for people leaving their country for America to bring balls of yarn with them, leaving the loose ends with relatives on the pier. Slowly, as the ship pulled away, the ball would begin to unwind and eventually the connection between the loved ones was broken, sometimes forever. If we'd given her a ball of yarn, Sergeant DeFilippo might have held on to the loose end as we dragged her down Interstate 40. Melissa and her crime scene unit is by far the most youthful we visited; Melissa is in her midthirties, and Frankie, Adrian, and Lauren are only in their twenties—mere babes in the police world. It will be interesting to see this young generation of CSIs and how they stand up to thirty more years of looking at and working the scenes of tragedies like the Nicole Giovanni case. Unfortunately, the world is not growing safer; don't be fooled by political speeches. This means that Melissa will probably have to string the bloodstains of many a young girl's bedroom. And through the passing years, just as in *The Shawshank Redemption* as Andy Dufresne changed the posters in his cell, Melissa will undoubtedly see blood on the next generation's teen idols. We just hope that she, and the rest of the young Union County crime scene investigators, will still be up to the challenge. God knows, the world can use more CSIs like them.

8

So Let It Be Written

NEW YORK CITY POLICE DEPARTMENT, NEW YORK

NEW YORK

NEW YORK

New York City is the single largest city in the United States and the second-largest in the world (Tokyo is number one). New York City is considered a major powerhouse in today's world economy. Founded in 1625, New York City is based on a system of five boroughs—The Bronx, Brooklyn, Manhattan, Queens, and Staten Island. The region was originally inhabited by the Lenape Indians and became the theater for several important battles during the Revolutionary War. The first presidential inauguration was held in New York City, and it was the capital of the country until 1790. The police department alone is larger than most cities, employing an astounding 37,038 people.

New York City. The Big Apple. Gotham. The city that never sleeps. Home to the Yankees, Broadway, Donald Trump, Wall Street; on September 11, 2001, home to the largest crime scene the world has ever known. Everything that happens or exists in New York City is simply bigger, brighter, and louder than anywhere else in the country. Population-wise, New York City is also the largest city in America, coming in at just over eight million people. But those who work within the city will tell you that including people who commute to or visit the city each day, and also counting the illegal immigrants, homeless people, and other unknowns, that number grows to more like eighteen million. In order to police a population that large, you need a virtual army. As of the most recent law enforcement census conducted by the Bureau of Justice Statistics, the New York City Police Department (NYPD) is composed of 37,038 full-time police officers—in army deployment standards, that's a corps. (Consider that the next largest police department, in Chicago, has 13,129 full-time officers.) Fifteen years ago, the NYPD had roughly three thousand homicides per year. Mayor Giuliani's policies brought crime down significantly, but the NYPD still works about eight hundred to nine hundred homicides per year—just under three per day. Unlike most of the other places we visited, seeing crime, murderous crime, was not going to be a problem in this city.

Our tires hummed across the George Washington Bridge into Queens. We had gotten up before daybreak to drive into New York from New Jersey because we were scheduled to meet Detective Larry Walsh at seven a.m. sharp. Unfortunately, we had gotten lost along the way. Good thing for us that Larry was also running late, and as if providence had intervened, Larry called us on his cell phone and was able to meet us on the bridge, so that we could follow him in. Let's just say that traffic laws and regulations are lost on Detective Walsh.

After jumping curbs and running through traffic lights irrespective of color, we arrived at Larry's office. We got out of our car to sunlight that disappeared when Larry the Giant got out of his. When we said everything is bigger in New York City, we meant it. Detective Larry Walsh is a big SOB. Huge. And scary. He's a heavy-metal-music-listening, earring-wearing giant who's very direct and uses the F-word as much as most people blink. He can carry the both of us, and unfortunately has, like a sack of potatoes—one in each arm. But in addition to his thick Bronx accent, his multiple ear piercings, and his omnipresent fleece vest, he has the heart of a teddy bear—a teddy bear itching to bitch-slap a mofo.

"How you doin'?" Larry grumbled deeply, as he gave each of us a big squeeze as soon as were out of our cars. Detective Walsh came crashing into our lives (he literally fell through the floor of a crime scene house) during Session VI at the National Forensic Academy—the only session in which we've ever had to evict someone for inappropriate actions. This person was a menace who aggravated the hell out of everyone and everything that he came in contact with. He was disgusting, vulgar, and a liar. Quite frankly, he was a horse's ass! And his classmates hated him. One day, while this person was acting typically

The authors with New York City Police Department
investigator Larry Walsh.
HALLCOX & WELCH, LLC

unpleasant, Larry came up beside us like an eclipse and said as loudly as he could—"Yo, you want I should bitch-slap the motherfucker in the ear?" We absolutely did, but we declined and instead went on to counsel the jackass for the umpteenth time. Eventually, we expelled him, to the chagrin of everyone who wanted to see that bitch-slap thing to completion.

Queens is home to the crime scene unit for all of New York City. The unit is composed of fifty men and women who respond to all sexual assaults, pattern crimes, and homicides that occur in New York. Each borough has its own evidence collection team for processing crimes that fall into other categories. The prevailing belief across the country is that the larger the police department, the more money it has, and thus the better off it is. This is hardly the case. New York officers' starting salaries are way below those of other large agencies. In addition, many surrounding counties have plenty of money (a strong recruiting incentive) to attract officers away from NYPD. "Janitors and teachers make more than we do," Larry said as he led us onto the floor where he worked. "None of us can afford to live in the city." Larry had driven all the way in from Long Island earlier that morning. To put it in perspective, the top pay for a NYPD officer puts him or her at about $65,588 per year. Even with the current pay raise the NYPD received in 2008, nearby Nassau County, on the other hand, tops out at $92,000. Suffolk County is $98,000.

The tight budget affects more than just an officer's salary. The perception most people have of a CSI unit is of some really high-tech place with stainless steel tables, microscopes, and all of the fancy whizgigs that money can buy. Unfortunately, that couldn't be any further from the truth. What we saw looked more like Barney Miller's office from thirty years ago—all Larry needed was a rotary phone and he'd be set. "We ain't got nuthin'," one of the guys said, after being introduced to us. They have computers, but they are not hooked up to the e-mail system, nor are they on a server that would allow them to share files. They have digital cameras, but they are not compatible with the computers they have, so they don't use them. Seeing the NYPD reminded us of stories of how Rome just grew too big to keep up with itself, with the outlying parts of the Roman Empire dying off first. The crime scene unit at NYPD is on the outskirts of a dying empire.

We sat with Larry and some of the rest of the guys in his unit for a while, drinking coffee and chatting about the television version of crime scene investigation. "What do you think about the show *CSI: New York*?" we asked the three guys sitting around the table.

"I only watched that shit once," Larry began, leaning over in his chair, pointing his behemoth finger in our direction. "And all I saw was them trying to find a rat who ate a fuckin' bullet. Getthefuckouttahere! How youse gonna find one rat in New York City? We gots millions a rats!"

"Did anyone from the show come here and see what it is that you guys do?" we timidly asked, now afraid to talk anymore about the show.

245

"Yeah, they were here for one day," one of the other guys answered. "One day, and they said, this ain't gonna make good TV."

"Do you guys like any of the CSI type of shows?" we asked.

"Yeah, *Dexter*," was the overwhelming response. What a shocker. The favorite show of the boys in blue is about a serial killer who's a forensic bloodstain analyst during the day, but who employs his own style of vigilante justice, limiting his killing to only bad guys. You gotta love New York.

Our plan for the day was to have Larry escort us around the city, visiting crime scenes being worked throughout the different boroughs. That is, if there were any. "Do you think they'll be any callouts?" we asked Larry sarcastically, as we looked through hundreds of his grisly crime scene photos. Before he could even respond to our question, a call came in to the precinct that a body had been found.

"So let it be written, so let it be done," Larry said, in that deep, Rocky-esque voice. Larry is fond of that biblical quote, though his version comes from the Metallica song "Creeping Death." When we had asked Larry months earlier whether we could visit him and see what his life was like as a CSI in New York City, his answer had been the same—"So let it be written, so let it be done." It's sort of his metal mantra.

We hurried down the back entrance of the building to where Larry's crime scene vehicle was parked. It was an old, beat-up Ford Explorer that made the run-down cars cabbies drive look like Cadillacs, in sharp contrast to the brand-new vehicle that the Union County folks were using just a few miles across the river. "This probably won't be much of a scene," Larry said, backing out of his spot wildly, as if he'd done this a thousand times before.

"How long have you been on the force?" we asked, scrambling to put on seat belts that turned out to not even work.

"Seventeen long years and six with the unit," Larry replied, making an illegal left U-turn on red, from the far left lane, in a police car with no blue lights.

"Um, Larry, do you always drive like this?" we asked, now really afraid for our lives.

"People in New York don't respect cops," Larry said indignantly. "Down south they still do, and even some out west, but not here. A cop here can look at a guy dealing in the street and the dealer will yell, 'What the fuck you looking at?' Used to be, you got something for being a cop. Now, there's no perks, no respect, no nuthin'. All we got left is running a red light or two."

After about fifteen minutes of "driving however you want," accumulating enough traffic points to keep thirty people off the road forever, we arrived at our first New York City crime scene. We drove right up to the tape and rolled out like we owned the place. "Yo Larry, what's up?" one of the guys yelled. As we found out, one of Detective Walsh's nicknames is "Larry Love." And everybody does love him.

"Whaddya got?" Larry asked, from the other side of the tape.

"Eh, a dead guy with his pants down around his ankles," the CSI replied to Larry. We arrived just after the body had been zipped into the body bag and placed in the medical examiner's van.

"These are friends from Tennessee," Larry said, introducing us as if we were at his house for dinner and not at a murder scene. We talked at length with the guys and gals working the scene, but there wasn't much to it. From the evidence they'd collected and the way the body had looked, it appeared to be a crime of passion between two lovers. In other words, "a fuck and dump," as somebody was heard to exclaim. The shift working the scene was the night shift, just finishing up their work that had lasted into the next morning. They had responded to eight homicides in just over twenty-four hours. That's as many homicides as most communities have in a year.

After a few minutes another call came in: Shots fired. We jumped into the car and sped to the next scene. When we got close, we turned down a street that looked more like a very wide alley, with businesses lined down each side. At the end of the street, we could see the crime scene tape that had been put up, right next to what appeared to be a car-detailing shop. Larry drove right under the crime scene tape toward where the detectives were standing. And they were a sight to behold. Four men all dressed to the nines, each with an ankle-length wool trench coat and slicked-back dark hair, and every one with a cell phone glued to his ear. It was like a quorum of Harvey Keitels huddled up in the street, and one of the few times it seems Hollywood got it right.

As we accompanied our brute of a tour guide up to the men in coats, each began flipping their cell phones down to give Larry some love. "Larry Love!" they hollered out to him as we approached the crime scene tape. With the pleasantries finished, Larry asked what was going on. "We got a hommy [homicide]; looks like a mob hit," one of the Keitels said as we watched blood literally run down the sidewalk and into the street. The CSI unit was busy processing the scene, photographing bullet ricochets, and collecting shell casings: evidence not typically left behind in a mob hit. In fact, there usually isn't any evidence left at a mob hit.

"Did anybody see anything?" we naively asked, looking at the dozens of people who lined the street watching the cops do their jobs.

"Nah, they're all wiseguys," Keitel number two snapped. Translation—they're all connected to the mob, so naturally, nobody saw nuthin'. The detectives had already worked out some connections between a couple of mobsters, narrowing down who they'd probably be looking for. But then before anyone could do anything, the trench-coat-clad detectives received another call.

A baby had been brought in to the morgue early that morning; it was thought to be a SIDS death. Yet just a few minutes into her examination, the medical examiner realized that it was no SIDS death; it was a homicide. "Another hommy," the lead Keitel said, flipping his cell phone shut. "The ME's doing the cut as we speak." In other words, the medical examiner was conducting the autopsy. With that, the four detectives jumped immediately into their cars, inviting us and Larry along to check it out.

The morgue was just around the corner from where the mob hit had occurred. It was essentially like any other morgue—old, dank, and overrun with sickeningly sweet smells. We found our way through the catacombs of rooms until we stumbled across the detectives and the ME, at work. The morgue is a terrible place no matter what city it is. No matter how anal retentive a medical examiner is with regard to cleaning, there are always bits of flesh in virtually every nook and cranny, remnants of death gone by. And it's very, very wet from the washing of the bodies and the squeegeeing of the diluted blood-water mix as it goes down the drain. We entered into the morgue just as the tech was dragging a freshly Y-incisioned cadaver off the autopsy table and back onto the gurney. Unfortunately for us, the gurney was much lower than the table, and the tech was much smaller than the cadaver (meaning she had to struggle a bit), so the body came down with a flop and a splash, and our faces were spattered with a fine mist of diluted, bloody death sweat.

To our right, the four horsemen huddled around the autopsy table where the baby lay, talking with the medical examiner, who looked suspiciously like Brigitte Nielsen. The ME invited us right into the midst of the conversation, which centered on the three-month-old infant's skull. "See, look here," she said, peeling back the flesh of the skull. She allowed us to move forward to see what she was talking about. "Hundreds and hundreds of tiny fractures," the ME continued. "Not a SIDS death." The tiny infant's body lay there, revealing a savage beating at someone's hands.

"Fuckin' shame," Keitel number three chimed in.

It was a shame. It has been our experience that most adult murders happen at night and are usually reported at night. Babies, on the other hand, almost always turn up dead first thing in the morning. All too often, angry husbands or pissed-off boyfriends, annoyed by a baby's crying, lose their tempers and react violently. Then the mothers bring in the baby the next morning, telling everyone who will listen that they "found the baby not moving when I got up," hoping that the hospital will think it's SIDS. Most don't realize that babies, just like adults, get a complete autopsy when the cause of death is unknown.

"Doc, take a picture of her just like that," the lead detective told the ME, regarding the infant. "I want them to see what they did." The detectives were already preparing for their investigation and interrogation of the parents, wanting to show them the picture of the autopsied infant to show them what they had done to her.

"We got the parents at the PD now," one of the Keitels said. "We'll see what they say." The photograph was snapped, and the ME readjusted the baby's head. Amazingly, she looked perfect. No bruising, no swelling, no nothing. She looked like a toy baby doll sitting on a stainless steel table. Without an autopsy, no one would ever have been the wiser about what the baby had endured. "Pleasure to meet youse guys; enjoy New York." And with that, the four trench-coated detectives vanished from our lives forever.

. . .

Noon approached as we left the morgue. Lunchtime. We have no idea what it is, but something primal happens in the body when it's around death for long periods of time. Unbelievable hunger almost always occurs in morgues. Our experience has been that the urge is even worse around decomposing bodies. It must have something to do with the body saying, "Hey, yoo-hoo, hello, you're not dead; eat something!" So we grabbed a sandwich at one of Larry's favorite haunts down in Brooklyn.

"What have you been up to?" we asked Larry, with our sandwiches in hand.

"Oh, I just worked a fire death," he responded. "A guy down in the city had been set on fire repeatedly, and then put out, and then set on fire again, just to torture him. Eventually, they sat the guy in a chair, duct taped his arms so they couldn't move and his head completely so he couldn't breathe, and set him on fire by lighting a bag of Kingsford charcoal." He paused. "It was all over drugs."

As we drove back to the department, we mentioned that we'd seen Larry in *People* magazine. "Oh yeah, the bouncer;

you saw that?" Detective Walsh had made a little splash in *People* magazine when he worked the homicide scene of female victim Imette St. Guillen. Darryl Littlejohn is the bouncer of the club she was last seen at, and has been accused of murdering the graduate student from John Jay College. "That guy knew what he was doing," Larry said, driving crazily back to Queens. "He was a scumbag."

· · ·

The case began when an anonymous 911 call came in to the NYPD that a body had been spotted lying on the side of the road near Spring Creek Park in Brooklyn, New York. There, police found the nude and almost unidentifiable body of Imette St. Guillen wrapped in a bedspread, her hands and feet tightly bound. A sock had been placed into her mouth and taped in place with clear shipping tape. She had claw marks, gouges, and other lacerations indicative of a sexual homicide. Her assailant had meant not only to kill but to torture her.

Allegedly, Darryl Littlejohn, a bouncer at a local nightclub, had had a disagreement with St. Guillen earlier that night. And some at the club say they saw the two of them together, arguing later in the evening. That's part and parcel of why he was developed as a suspect. After his arrest, he consented to a DNA swab, and laboratory tests confirmed that it matched DNA found on St. Guillen's body. Though it's a wonder there was any to match at all. "He cleaned the girls up that he raped," Larry said, clearly agitated by the thought. Purportedly, Littlejohn had raped before—afterward showering his victims, using soap, brushing their teeth, changing their clothes, and washing their mouths out with mouthwash before turning them back out into the street. Or he would dump their dead bodies along the side of the road, as he did with St. Guillen.

"Did you work the scene?" we asked, meaning when St. Guillen had been found.

"No," Larry said, "I went back after the initial crime scene had been worked to collect more evidence regarding the other rapes." Along with the DNA, other evidence helped provide the key links between Littlejohn and St. Guillen. The tape that covered her mouth had trace fibers consistent with fibers from Littlejohn's home. In addition, unusual fibers from jackets found in Littlejohn's home were also found on the tape across St. Guillen's mouth. Eyewitnesses reported seeing Littlejohn's van turning around in the neighborhood where her body was later found. All of the evidence added up to a three-count indictment against Darryl Littlejohn. The case is still awaiting trial.

"Why do you stay and work here, Larry?" we asked him as we sat around the lunch table. We had heard very few reasons to want to be employed as a crime scene investigator in New York City. They get very little support, the pay is terrible, and there's a lot of violent crime.

"I grew up here; I've lived here all my life," Larry replied with feeling to our question. That's the way it is with a lot of the cops with the NYPD. It's a feeling; a belief in something bigger. It's certainly not the money or the fame. Most guys on the force have to take side jobs just to make ends meet. And Larry's no different. He's the bodyguard for the lead singer of Skid Row—one Sebastian Bach. "I even sat next to the copycat Zodiac killer in high school," Larry said. "That crazy guy painted his fingernails black back then; I knew he was a weirdo." Where else in the world can you go to high school with an infamous copycat serial killer and grow up to be a bodyguard for a 1990s metal band? Only in New York, kids, only in New York.

"We certainly don't work for the brass," Larry said indignantly, flexing his giant muscled arms. Larry has ruffled more than a few feathers during his seventeen years with the department—but not among the people he works with directly. Each and every person we bumped into—whether another CSI or a detective from a different precinct—all said the same thing: "If something happened to me or my family, I'd want Larry to work the scene." That speaks volumes about Larry and what he knows. "One supervisor said I was a diamond in the rough," Walsh told us as we were sitting in the break room of the unit. "I have a photographic memory," Larry Love said, rubbing his stubble. And he's telling the truth. He remembers vivid details about every training and every situation he has ever been in. That kind of recall makes him a perfect CSI. It also makes him the perfect target.

"It's hard to soar like an eagle when you fly with turkeys," Larry said. Larry's abilities, coupled with his uninhibited way of speaking his mind, have not made him a favorite son with some of his bosses. The department is so big that by default there's often a huge disconnect between the administrators and the worker bees. This problem is exacerbated in the CSI unit, where the disconnect involves more than just knowledge of what is going on in the department. It involves knowledge of forensic science.

"They don't know what the fuck we do," one of the CSIs said, coming by to get a cup of coffee in the break room. "They think we do magic." Indeed, the CSI Effect doesn't happen only in courtrooms. There is a CSI Effect among administrators in many police departments across the country. We heard stories of guys not in the unit asking the CSIs to do ridiculous things, like taking a swab from a suspect and touching it to a cell phone to get his identity. We also heard stories of brass visiting scenes and becoming overwhelmed when some of the simplest pieces of equipment were used, such as a laser measuring device. Many of the older guys who have been promoted up through the ranks over the years are simply afraid of the science of crime scene investigation. It's an attitude of "I don't know, and I don't want to know." And fear breeds antagonism in certain people.

"Sometimes they come down to the scene when there's media," Larry said, cleaning up his lunch. "And they ask stupid questions or make stupid requests. Any question they ask me, like how do I know something, I just tell them I put it to the Moulage test. They don't know what the fuck I'm talking about, but they can't question it or they'll look stupid. So they just nod their heads and go away."

With lunch all but digested, Larry took us on a tour of the NYPD crime laboratory. Most states have a crime lab for the entire state, and some bigger states have more than one. But the NYPD has its own lab in the same building as the CSI unit, just one floor up. Most CSIs would give anything for that proximity. Day in and day out, investigators all over the country have to liaison with lab personnel, many not in the same city, regarding evidence that they have collected and sent to the lab for analysis. Yet in New York City, until the day we visited Larry, he had never been up to the lab—never. He knew no one; no one knew him. The two entities might as well have been a thousand miles apart. Once he submits the evidence that he has collected, he moves on to the next case—more proof that being a bigger department does not necessarily mean being better.

Though Larry had not arranged for us to take a tour, the police brotherhood provided us with the opportunity to visit the lab, which was as state-of-the-art as crime labs get. Nearly every process and application imaginable could be performed in the city's laboratory, including microscopy, toxicology, and ballistics. The other unique thing about the NYPD lab was the amount of space dedicated solely to housing drug evidence. More space was dedicated to drugs than most labs have in total space. They had also recently confiscated a large amount of marijuana—a couple of pallets' worth to be exact, which is a common occurrence in New York City. We each developed a contact buzz before we finished our tour.

Lining the interior of the drug evidence area was shelf after shelf of every conceivable type of drug that had been collected as evidence at the scene of a crime: Ecstasy, heroin, LSD, Vicodin, OxyContin, ketamine. Whatever your poison, it's probably there. They had even confiscated tons of trial-size prescription drugs such as diazepam. The amount of drug evidence processed by the city was simply amazing.

As we rounded the corner from the drug evidence area, we came to the ballistics part of the lab. These areas in crime labs are always interesting, with hundreds of guns skewered on pegboard for display and easy retrieval for testing. Guns that are confiscated as part of a crime are kept on file as examples for future cases. The most interesting guns are always found in here. Homemade guns of every kind, and any kind of foreign gun imaginable, hang in the locker. Outside the evidence room was a glass case, a museum of sorts, displaying the weirdest and most famous guns that had been obtained over the years. Included in this gruesome collection of weapons was the .38-caliber pistol that Mark David Chapman used to kill John Lennon, as well as the .44-caliber handgun that David Berkowitz, a.k.a. "Son of Sam," used in his rash of serial killings in the late 1970s.

With the tour of the forensic lab over, we went back downstairs to Larry's cubicle to see some of the crime scene photos he'd taken while working on the tragic Staten Island Ferry crash that occurred in 2003. It was the worst tragedy in the hundred-plus years the ferry had been in operation. Larry worked the entire scene, documenting what had happened after the ferry violently slammed into the Staten Island Pier. "It's just another scene," Larry said of his work. Eleven people were killed, many dismembered or otherwise torn to pieces as the captain of the ferry slept at the wheel. The pictures were too gruesome to look at; most of the victims were unrecognizable as human beings, looking more like horrible Halloween costumes. Most CSIs that we have worked with over the years are able to separate themselves from their jobs. Otherwise, they would not be able to cope with all of the horror and human tragedy they are exposed to. Larry, though, and many others from NYPD, seem to have reached an even higher level of separation, which stems directly from the tragedy of September 11.

At about the same time we were looking at the pictures and going over the ferry case, a large crowd had gathered outside and was wrapping around the entire precinct. With the windows open, chants of "Kill the pigs who killed our kids" could be heard echoing off the outside façade of the building. The protesters were blocking the streets, the entranceways, and the exits. We were essentially trapped inside the building by an angry mob.

"What's going on?" we asked, nervous about the events outside.

"It's over the shooting of Sean Bell," said Larry, obviously frustrated by the events unfolding. We were less than a month from the shooting when the protest occurred. On November 25, 2006, Sean Bell and two of his friends were stormed with a hail of police gunfire after exiting a strip club in Queens. The trio

BEHIND THE YELLOW TAPE

had been celebrating Sean's last day as a bachelor; he was due to be married the following day. In all, fifty bullets were fired into the group, killing Sean and wounding his two friends.

"Why were so many bullets fired?" we asked of the CSIs who had gathered around to hear the protest.

"One of the cops thought he saw a gun," one of the group offered up.

"When I first got into police work, all I used to do was chase down people with guns," Larry commented, his thick accent deepening as the day went on. "I would be undercover and drive a car that looked like it belonged in a bad neighborhood, windows tinted dark black, and when we'd see a gun, we'd bounce and run after them, trying to get the illegal guns off the street.

"It was all a game—a dangerous game. Many times, the gun would be tossed and it would do the 'Brooklyn Bounce' before we could even get to it." The *Brooklyn Bounce* simply meant that the gun was picked up and gone somewhere else fast.

Most law enforcement officers go twenty or thirty years without ever having to fire their weapon or even removing their gun from the holster, except to qualify at the range once or twice per year. Larry's an exception. He has used his gun, and often. So have many other NYPD officers. But fifty bullets seemed very excessive in this case. "But why fifty, Larry?" we asked candidly.

"Well, the old saying goes, better to be tried by twelve than carried by six," he replied, with a shoulder shrug.

As the sun set on our day in New York City and the angry mob dispersed into the cold night, we went to dinner with Detective Larry Walsh at his favorite eatery in Queens, the Rincon Montane Restaurant. It was like going to dinner with Norm from *Cheers*. He was a regular.

We were ushered to a small table near the back of the restaurant along the far wall, where Ramon, manager of the restaurant, presided over us as if we were royalty. The only thing Larry loves more than Spanish food is Spanish women; he greeted every waitress who came by with "How you doin'?" Though we were handed menus, Larry took control of the night, ordering in Spanish for both of us.

"You know, we had this endless wipe not long ago in Brooklyn," Larry said.

"Endless wipe?" we asked, no idea what he was referring to.

"Yeah, an endless wipe; working a crime scene that never ends," Larry said, motioning with his hands. New Yorkers have terminology for everything. But the most original was *space case*, which refers to a poor guy who gets sandwiched between the subway train and the platform. Larry's endless wipe had been another one of those "I smell something funny" cases. When emergency services arrived on the scene at the apartment, the bedroom door had been sealed off with towels stuffed under the door and decomp fluids leaking under the doorjamb. They had to knock the door down, and when they did, they witnessed a woman jumping out the window and fleeing down the fire escape. Inside, they discovered a male in the bloat stage of decomposition, purging out the anus, leeching fluids throughout the apartment. "Dude had overdosed," Larry said. The medical examiner determined that no foul play was involved. They eventually discovered that the woman had been the dead guy's girlfriend, and she'd been mopping up the body fluids, pouring pine-scented cleaner everywhere, and hanging up air fresheners by the dozens, hoping to cover the smell. "She kept climbing back into the apartment through the windows to sell the dude's shit for dope," Larry said, gulping his beer.

"Did you catch her?" we asked Larry as the food arrived.

"No," he responded, while making sure everyone's order was correct, speaking fluent Spanish to the waiters. "Her only crime would be grand larceny if the amount she stole was enough. We got bigger shit to work on than that; we can't work every petty crime."

Just as Larry finished speaking, a guy came in off the street with a messenger bag hanging from his shoulder. He moved from table to table, until he reached ours. "DVDs?" he said, offering up his selection. This guy had every new movie imaginable, even movies just released over the weekend, all for sale at five bucks a pop. He also had hard-core porno for sale, "if you're interested." Larry motioned for him to move on and the guy did, never having a clue that he had just offered an NYPD officer illegal movies. "That shit just ain't worth our time," Larry said, digging into his heaping plate of sautéed garlic and plantains.

"Did that case smell worse than the Body Farm?" we asked Larry.

"I didn't think the Body Farm was bad," Larry said, shrugging his shoulders. "The worst smell I ever smelled was at Ground Zero."

"Well." We gulped. "You've avoided that conversation all day; anything you wanna say about your experience there?"

Larry ate a bite of chicken, then garlic and plantain, then he bent his head down again and spoke reverently. "I never want to relive the smell," Larry began quietly. "Pulverized concrete, fiberglass, water, and bodies—never been anything on Earth like it." Larry had been part of the first groups to arrive, going into the first tower that was hit.

"I had just dropped my kid off," Larry said, taking a big swig of beer. "When the second plane hit, I knew—we all knew—that it was a terrorist attack." Larry had been standing at Ground Zero when the second tower collapsed.

The first couple of days after September 11 were complete chaos. Nobody had taken charge, and everybody was sort of doing their own thing, trying to rescue somebody, anybody. Then, after a couple of days, most realized that the work had changed from rescue to recovery. That's when the CSI units really got involved. "Each body part that we found got tagged and entered into a Global Positioning System," he continued slowly. He then segued to the Pennsylvania plane crash site, led by emotion and a few Spanish beers. He's not completely convinced by the official story of what happened there. "That engine was something like five hundred yards behind where the plane was found. Something else did that."

As quickly as he had begun talking about 9/11, he stopped. For several minutes he just stared at the jumbo TV, drinking his bottomless glass of beer. We each picked at the remnants of our spicy food, holding back garlic and rice burps. After talking for hours about crime, New York, 9/11, and nothing in particular, the time had come for us to leave our Larry Love. He drove us back to our car, his radio blaring the sounds of a new Sebastian Bach song. He was en route soon to China, at the request of Mr. Bach, to do what he does best: guard bodies. With a final hug, a gentle pickup off the ground, and a few tears, we said our good-bye to Larry Love so we could catch a few winks back at our hotel before our long drive home the next morning.

The next morning, we watched the *Today* show down in the common area of the hotel with the other vacationers, businessmen, and the like. The scrolling marquee whizzed by the bottom of the television screen with weather reports, box scores, and an up-to-the-minute look at the Dow Jones. Sandwiched somewhere between sports and weather was the mention of a three-month-old baby who had been murdered by her father in the Bronx the day before. He had confessed to the killing and had been arrested. "Who the fuck would do that to a kid?" someone in the room said. Other than the NYPD and the medical examiner's office, we were among the few people on the planet who knew the intimate details of what had transpired.

The previous night, Larry's partner had been sent to work the scene at the parents' house, looking for any evidence that might show foul play. There was nothing tremendously out of place or suspicious—except for a perfectly rounded indentation in the wallboard, where the father had crushed his daughter's head. "She wouldn't stop crying," he later told the police.

We had had the privilege of seeing what the ME saw, hearing what the detectives knew, and knowing what the CSIs had found. But in a city like New York, a city ranging anywhere from eight million to eighteen million residents, it's virtually impossible for any one person on the criminal justice continuum to get that viewpoint. The father had confessed to the murder, which more than likely meant there would be no jury trial, so it's possible that none of the players would ever know the whole story. With so much crime every day, they'd all be back to their respective autopsy tables, trench coats, and fingerprint brushes. In a sense, crime scene investigation in New York is like working in a huge Corvette factory, where the guy who makes the starters never sees the completed car—he just keeps churning out starter after starter after starter. Having that myopic view is sometimes problematic because it's easy to lose sight of the bigger picture. The never-ending job of working death takes its toll, and the reality of the job can sometimes get lost—and it's all in the perspective that each keeps. The guy on the assembly line, when asked what he does, can either answer blandly that he makes starters or proudly, and accurately, say that he builds Corvettes. Larry, the ME, and the Keitels could answer that

BEHIND THE YELLOW TAPE

question, focusing on what their individual jobs are. But a better answer, and a better answer for every entity of the criminal justice system throughout the country, is to answer the question proudly—"I am a builder of Corvettes; I am a solver of crime." And being a solver of crime is about as worthwhile a job as there is. So let it be done.

9

Back to the Future!

ANYTOWN, USA

Shots fired, shots fired!" the caller screams to the 911 operator. The operator takes the information and immediately calls the Anytown Police Department, sending the first responding officers to the address of the house where the call came from. The officers rush to the scene with blue lights flashing and sirens blaring. As soon as they arrive, they draw their weapons from their holsters and approach the house carefully, methodically checking every door, every window, and every corner—making sure the perp is gone and the scene is safe. Within minutes, the officers see what appear to be bloody shoe prints on the sidewalk leading away from the house and blood pooling out from under the front door. The responding officers, believing that they probably have a murder scene on their hands, call their regional laboratory, requesting the assistance of the Crime Scene Response Team (CSRT).

Shortly thereafter, the CSRT arrives in its fully equipped

crime scene truck, decked out with all of the latest and greatest forensic equipment. This truck also comes complete with satellite communications and UHF wireless transmission capabilities for constant and real-time communication with the laboratory. These communications are broadcast on the newly acquired 700 MHz frequency named the Wireless Forensic Telecommunications Network (WFTN), once used by the television broadcast industry. UHF information sent wirelessly at this frequency can easily penetrate walls and buildings and can be sent long distances—all things that traditional Wi-Fi cannot do. By the time the team arrives on the scene, the crime scene response commander has been alerted and has assigned a crime scene case manager to oversee the entire case from processing the crime scene to getting the case to the courtroom. The case manager, who stays back at the laboratory, is a seasoned veteran with years of practical casework experience. He takes his post behind a fifty-inch high-definition plasma screen television where he can see and hear what is happening at the crime scene in real time.

On arrival, the team members gather all of the information they can from the responding officers. Before they begin to process the scene, they all confer in the truck, with the case manager assigning duties via the WFTN. As they dress themselves in the newest anticontaminating PPE (personal protective equipment), a team member prepares headsets with microphones for everyone to wear while the scene is being processed. Thus, team members are always in constant communication among themselves and with the case manager at the lab.

At the house, the seven-person response team begins its assault on the crime scene. Five people process the scene, searching for, photographing, and collecting evidence. Another person is in charge of being the videographer, recording everything at the scene and transmitting the live video feed back to the plasma screen at the lab. The seventh member of the team remains in the command center within the crime scene truck, managing the multimedia communication system.

The photographer of the team begins taking digital pictures immediately. Through the use of a wireless SD memory card within the camera, the photographs are uploaded from the camera to a computer back at the laboratory. Of particular photographic interest at this scene are two pieces of evidence: a fingerprint that was just developed on the frame of the doorjamb and the bloody shoe prints on the sidewalk that seem to lead away from the scene. As the pictures of the fingerprint and shoe prints are taken, they are instantaneously transmitted to the lab, where the case manager receives them. The case manager downloads the photographs and adjusts them in Adobe Photoshop, a digital imaging program, to bring out the best details in the photographs of the evidence. The manager then e-mails the photo of the fingerprint down to the latent prints section of the lab, where it is immediately uploaded into AFIS, the nationwide fingerprint database. The photo of the shoe print is submitted into the known shoe pattern database that contains tens of thousands of different patterns of footwear.

As the CSRT continues to process the crime scene, the

DNA specialist of the group begins to swab the blood found outside the scene, collecting samples and placing some of what is collected into a newly created device called "DNA on a chip." This device, not much bigger than a dime, can sort the DNA strands by size and determine a profile for the sample. Within ten minutes, the chip confirms that two different people shed blood at the scene—a Hispanic female, who is the victim, and an unknown male Caucasian "person of interest." The findings are submitted back to the lab, where the case manager will take the information and begin his collaboration with investigators at the Anytown Police Department.

The other members of the team continue processing the inside of the house, combing the dwelling for anything that may be evidence. "What's that?" comes through on everyone's earpieces. The case manager, who's been watching the team work the scene from his lab, has seen something on the screen and directs the videographer over to the broken window where a piece of fiber, possibly from the suspect, hangs in the shards of broken glass. The fiber is collected by the team.

The team continues to work the scene, communicating throughout with the case manager at the lab. They use laptop computers called *tablet PCs* that allow them to write their scene notes, draw their scene sketches, and enter evidence into a log, all by writing on the computer screen. This technology eliminates writing notes on paper and having to transcribe them back at the office. All of the evidence that is collected and packaged is labeled with a bar code and scanned into the system for laboratory submission. The case manager consults with the team on what pieces of evidence have the most probative case merit and ultimately decides to submit only those that are determined to be the most relevant to the lab. Because investigators can determine at the scene which pieces of evidence are most important to the case, the lab will not have to spend time processing items with less evidentiary value, thus eliminating the "everything but the kitchen sink" mentality that has traditionally overwhelmed laboratories.

Within eight hours the entire crime scene has been processed. While the team worked the scene, the lab scientists were already running tests on the evidence that was collected to help investigators with their search for the suspect in question. A positive match comes back in AFIS with the name of a male Caucasian, thus confirming the DNA-on-a-chip field sequencing. The shoe-pattern database also identifies the shoe print as coming from a New Balance tennis shoe. All of that information—name, race, even type of shoe—are critical in finding a suspect, and within hours that information has been given to the police department investigators. Before one full day has passed, the suspect is arrested, still wearing those same bloody New Balance shoes.

• • •

Sounds too good to be true, doesn't it? Too much like a Hollywood sci-fi flick, involving the creation of a flux capacitor and a wild trip in a used, plutonium-powered DeLorean. But it could be the *crime scene of the future*. In this day and age, crime scene investigation is usually a very low-tech affair, lacking continuity between the crime scene and the crime lab. And worst of all, forensic science usually plays a very small role in the actual investigation. By the time the laboratory analyst receives the evidence, analyzes the pieces, and sends them back to the investigating department (which is a time frame of roughly six months), the investigators already have a suspect in mind and quite probably have already made an arrest. The prosecutor then uses the evidence that was analyzed to either corroborate or refute the testimony of the accused. For a long time, forensic science has been a prosecutorial tool, providing the evidentiary ammunition for the prosecutor to go to court. The crime scene we just described could be the future of forensic criminal investigations.

"I've always thought that forensic science should be an investigative tool," forensic scientist Jeff Gurvis explains to us, on a cold and blustery day in Knoxville, Tennessee. Jeff has come to town to teach bloodstain pattern analysis at the academy. But this is only one of the many forensic hats that Jeff wears. Jeff is the lab director of a newly envisioned forensic laboratory. Though still in its early planning stages, this one-of-a-kind private, full-service laboratory could revolutionize forensic science. "That's what it should be all about," Jeff continued, "helping and aiding the investigation. Just think, if everything was in real time, everything is still hot, everybody is still very interested; the first forty-eight hours is the most crucial, right, so forensic science should help in that time frame."

The first forty-eight hours *are* the most crucial part of criminal investigations; after forty-eight hours, the odds of solving a case are drastically reduced, nearly cut in half. With many lab tests taking months to complete, the investigative value of the forensic evidence collected at the scene is diminished and, in many cases, nonexistent. According to Jeff, "Forensic science provides little to no impact during the first forty-eight hours because of backlogs, how things are organized, et cetera."

Because of his unique background, Jeff confidently states that he has been in more forensic laboratories than anyone in the United States. Jeff began his career by getting a master's degree in forensic science from Michigan State University, followed by an MBA from DePaul University. His career has been eclectic. He has been part of a state crime lab, worked many forensic cases, and taught in countless places, such as the FBI National Academy and the NFA. He currently works for the Porter Lee Corporation installing laboratory software known as The Beast in labs across America. The Beast is an integrated evidence-tracking system for police departments and crime laboratories. In simple terms, it is an electronic way to track and submit forensic evidence collected at the scene. These unique educational and practical forensic backgrounds, not to mention his age (he's only thirty-six), have made Jeff one of the young guns in the forensic community. This background and open-mindedness has led him to view things differently from many of his older counterparts.

"A lot of the law enforcement community scoff at the show

CSI and discount it completely," Jeff goes on to say. "I've always thought that some of the tools and some of the ways things are done on *CSI* should be something to strive for—they are definitely possible, and the technology, for the most part, exists."

Indeed, all of the technology used in our "crime scene of the future" does exist today. The wireless SD card can be purchased at Wal-Mart. The real-time, high-definition streaming video already occurs all over the Internet, twenty-four hours a day, seven days a week. A footwear database, a concept that is being heavily championed in England, exists as well. One database in particular, called Solemate, was created by the U.K. laboratory Foster & Freeman and can currently be found in a few laboratories in the United States. The wireless UHF band will become available in 2009 as broadcast television goes completely digital. Even the DNA on a chip is a real device that is currently being perfected in laboratories such as the Y-12 National Laboratory and Harvard—though, admittedly, it is still in the early testing phase. In many ways, the technology used in our futuristic crime scene is reminiscent of an episode right out of television. Hollywood often uses technologies that seem incredible or, at the very least, too good to be true—yet for all of the complaints directed at these types of shows, maybe, on some level, they've got some things right. One way that television may have improved on reality, much to our chagrin, is *CSI*'s Gil Grissom. He's the closest thing on television or otherwise akin to a forensic case manager—someone who follows the case from beginning to end and leads the team in all aspects of the investigation—and that's something desperately missing from today's approach to crime scene investigation.

"What's lacking in forensic science is that holistic view of crime scene work," Jeff began, just before we arrived at a local restaurant down on the Tennessee River. "The more experience you bring to the scene, whether they are physically there or remotely there, the more knowledge you have at your disposal and, thus, the more effective you will be.

"Currently, the practice of forensic science from crime scene to crime lab is a very disjointed affair. It is chopped into many disparate pieces that do not readily communicate with one another unless they have to," Jeff continued. The reality of crime scene investigation is not one of a technologically advanced unit, using all of what science has to offer, being managed holistically by a case manager with years of experience, following the case all the way from crime scene to crime lab to courtroom. Each participant on the forensic continuum is a virtual island. More often than not, the patrol officer must process a crime scene by himself as part of his other job duties, with low-tech or "no-tech" equipment—perhaps a fingerprint kit he's rarely, if ever, used—and then submit what he collects to a very high-tech laboratory. Here, the lab scientists can only use their vast scientific instruments based solely on what they have been sent, not ever fully understanding the nuances of the scene or even readily communicating with the officer who submitted it. The forensic disciplines within the lab won't talk to one another except to discuss what evidence needs to be analyzed by someone else. Labs themselves have become nothing more than assembly lines, taking evidence in and processing evidence out—though in most instances, the slow speed at which this assembly line is conducted would cause Henry Ford to turn over in his grave.

"And I know [from having done it myself] how long analysis of evidence should take," Jeff tells us.

"Okay, Jeff," we began our inquisition in between salads and biscuits, "how long would it take to analyze a sample of DNA if nothing else was going on?"

Jeff thought for a second and said, "Twenty-four hours, though I would allow thirty-six to double-check the results."

Thirty-six hours! We have talked to people in labs ourselves, and when we gave the same utopian scenario that we had posed to Jeff, the best answer we received was two weeks. Even at two weeks, with thousands of rape kits waiting to be analyzed in laboratory coolers and new cases coming in daily, the laboratory backlog will never end. Which means that rapists can go on raping and killers can go on killing, at least for six months, or in some cases (as we sometimes saw during our travels) indefinitely. Lord only knows how many serial killers' DNA sits unexamined in laboratories across America. An estimated fifty to a thousand serial killers are operating in the United States alone, and you can almost guarantee that at least one of them has his or her DNA just sitting on a shelf in a walk-in cooler somewhere, waiting to be analyzed.

And that's just issues within the laboratory. The whole

concept of crime scene investigation within a law enforcement agency has an inherent problem as well, which is that forensic science—or, more specifically, crime scene investigation—is not a career path per se. Traditionally, the CSI units' commanding officer will be someone who has been transferred in to manage that particular unit, but has never set foot on a crime scene or, at the most, had one day of training in forensics. "Why is that?" we asked Jeff.

"The reason," he stated, "is that most of your police chiefs, your superintendents, and other high-level figure heads, for them, forensic science is the lowest thing on the totem pole. Forensic science is not usually part of their knowledge base or their experience, and thus the farthest thing from their minds."

Unfortunately, that situation has come to be known within the law enforcement circle as dealing with the F.O.G. *F.O.G.*, better known as the "fucking old guy," is a phrase that we were introduced to on our travels around the country, and the F.O.G. almost always stands in the way of progress. Some personnel who reside within law enforcement agencies are notorious for lagging about twenty to twenty-five years behind the rest of the country when it comes to things such as management strategies and technological adaptation, preferring to invest in old-fashioned blue lights, sirens, and guns instead of new and advanced law enforcement tools. That's particularly true with regard to anything involving forensic science. We heard horror stories of how some bureaucrats don't understand the need for more fingerprint brushes or the necessity of moving away from

Polaroid cameras, even though the film alone costs the department in excess of $100,000 per year and won't even be available after early 2009—and perhaps much later. These decisions are not grounded in logic but based solely on fear—a fear of what they don't understand and a fear of becoming obsolete. To them, it's easier to maintain the status quo than to innovate or change, preferring to rely on the concept of "doing things the way they've always been done."

The problem is further exacerbated by the fact that investigators within the crime scene unit, if they are promoted, have to be promoted outside the unit and into patrol or another division within the agency because there is no upward mobility within the CSI unit. We've seen students, good students, come through the academy and go back to their departments—only to get promoted right out of their units. The unit then loses that forensic knowledge base and that training investment and has to start all over in replacing what they promoted out over and over and over again. It's a vicious cycle that is not easily remedied within the current structure of most law enforcement agencies. But that could all change soon.

Crime scene investigation has not always been a professional discipline. For years, the job of the CSI was performed by any cop who happened to be the one to collect the evidence. There was no training, no degree, no official title. This has begun to change within the past decade or so, with entire units dedicated to crime scene investigation, degree programs, and specialized training. Colleges and universities across the nation are adding forensic science and crime scene investigation as disciplines within their curriculum, and many are offering four-year degrees in those subjects. Some are even offering master's-level degrees as well. When Jeff graduated from Michigan State, the university had just about the only program offering a degree, particularly a master's degree, in forensic science. Now degree programs are springing up all over the country, with some of the best programs being offered at West Virginia University, Marshall University, the University of Alabama at Birmingham, George Washington University, and John Jay College of Criminal Justice. Soon we will be seeing these and other college graduates flooding the workforce with an advanced knowledge of forensic science and investigations that was once obtained only through years of experience on the job.

It is becoming more and more important for law enforcement agencies to recognize and understand the world in which we now live—or better still, the world in which we *will* live. The television show *CSI* has raised expectations, even if they are at times unreasonable, regarding what a crime scene unit and investigator should be able to perform. Many law enforcement agencies are also slowly starting to put a little more focus on crime scene investigation training, adding it to their police academies and sending officers to one-week and even ten-week training courses—something that was unthinkable less than ten years ago. It takes a big person to realize that things could be done better—and an even bigger person to seek out the help and training that the department needs.

The options for this help and training continue to grow. John Jay College of Criminal Justice is a leader in the professionalization of the CSI field. In February 2008 the college announced that it will be establishing a Crime Scene Academy— an international center for crime scene training for law enforcement professionals, undergraduate and graduate students, and the general public. This center, the first of its kind, is being made possible in part by a generous gift to John Jay by world-renowned author Patricia Cornwell.

The Crime Scene Academy at John Jay will be the first program of its kind to take a holistic approach to crime scene investigation. The program will add degree programs for college students, educate and assist law enforcement professionals, and even help elementary and middle school educators add forensic science to their curriculum. Other academies tend to focus only on professionals who are already in the field, but this one plans to educate everyone on the CSI continuum, including the general public, which is rare for law enforcement training. For centuries, law enforcement training and practices have traditionally been accessible only to those in the field, shielding the public from what goes on behind the yellow tape. This new academy intends to educate the public and hopefully arm juries with the knowledge they need to make informed decisions and eliminate the specter of the unknown when it comes to crime and crime scene investigation.

Texas State University at San Marcos is taking a different approach to enhancing the field of crime scene investigation. It is in the initial planning stages for a Forensic Research Facility very similar to the Body Farm at the University of Tennessee. This five-acre facility, part of the university's forensic anthropology program, will train both forensic scientists and law enforcement personnel in areas such as time since death and identifying human remains. Because the climate of Texas is so vastly different from that of eastern Tennessee, the data that comes out of this new forensic research facility will add tremendously to that which has been coming out of the Body Farm for the past thirty years.

All of these developments in technology, research, and education will surely have a tremendous impact in the world of forensic science—leading to innovative people, practices, techniques, and ideas. Simultaneous advancements in forensics should bring about a plethora of changes within the law enforcement community, not the least of which will be in the lab.

"So Jeff, what is your concept that's going to revolutionize the world of forensics?" we asked, somewhat jokingly; we've been needling Jeff for years about being the young guy with all the big ideas.

"Well, I had the idea back when I was in college," Jeff responded, ignoring our teasing and launching into a story of how, back when he was working on his MBA and volunteering at the Northern Illinois Crime Laboratory, he began devising a plan to develop the United States' first full-service private forensic laboratory—the National Forensic Support Laboratory. "This laboratory will serve, for the first time, the entire nation, in the core seven forensic disciplines—DNA, firearms, trace, drug chemistry, toxicology, latent fingerprints, and questioned documents," Jeff stated proudly. "It will be available to law enforcement agencies to give them an alternative to going to their local crime laboratory; for court systems to have independent testing done; for defense attorneys to have retesting done; for private investigators, insurance companies, corporate security firms, and the general public, thus providing forensic services to whoever needs it." And, almost as if he had already come up with a slogan for the lab, he finished his homily with the statement: "Because what we do inside the lab should not impact who's using us." In other words, whether it's the prosecution or the defense paying for the test, the results will always be the same. True science doesn't play favorites.

The idea, at its core, is not a novel one. Consider the whole DNA craze: At the moment DNA is all the rage, and because of its enormous popularity, private DNA laboratories have sprung up all across the country, offering their services to everyone from police departments trying to find the bad guy to suspicious, underwear-sniffing spouses trying to prove that a mate is being unfaithful. The reason—they want answers fast. "What about the other disciplines?" Jeff asks rhetorically. "Not every crime has DNA, and you have all of these other disciplines which may be of the same or even greater value than DNA. Thus you would have the same laboratory framework that exists within a state laboratory, but now take that out of the government's hands and put it into an independent environment that runs like a business. Then turnaround times would be faster and the quality would be higher, meeting the customers' needs. And we can help with the backlog too. State labs are already outsourcing their DNA to private DNA labs, but what about the other disciplines? We can help with those as well, catching the labs back up." Theoretically, the backlog could eventually be eliminated altogether with regional private support laboratories.

Jeff's idea has merits beyond simply creating an alternative lab to help with backlog, as well as independent analysis. For instance, not every case needs a specialist along the lines of an entomologist, or even a forensic anthropologist. We've been spoiled in Knoxville, Tennessee, with our access to the legendary Dr. Bill Bass and all his protégés still in the area. If a bone is found in the woods here, the police department can take it to an expert right away. But more often than not, a law enforcement agency does not have the luxury of a forensic anthropology expert at its disposal. We've heard off-the-record stories of skulls that were recovered when someone happened on them in the woods, but because of lack of access to an expert, they ended up fruitlessly passed around until they eventually became nothing more than a conversation piece within a department. Yet a private lab could provide that specialist at any moment. With just an overnight FedEx trip away, a forensic anthropologist could be analyzing the department's evidence the very next day. And although most states may not have enough cases to warrant creating an entire forensic anthropology department within the state laboratory, there certainly would be plenty of cases to justify maintaining one nationally. Once you take Jeff's laboratory model outside the government structure, the world becomes wide open, and a lab can make efficient use of several things, including economies of scale, because of this expansion. But the greatest advantage a laboratory outside the traditional government boundaries could bring is innovation—which brings us back to our crime scene of the future and the reality of real-time forensic investigation.

"Just think about it: real-time forensic investigation," Jeff enthused as we began to wind down our interview. "Why *not* provide forensic evidence during the first forty-eight hours?" Even we had not thought about how little forensic science actually helps in locating—rather than prosecuting—a suspect. We guess, like everyone else, we just took it for granted that DNA takes six months to run, and other analyses will get done when they get done. And no one questions it. Sometimes it just takes someone like Jeff to ask, "Why not?" before people begin to think about it differently and to take action.

We said our good-byes to our friend, who was headed to a lab in South Dakota to begin yet another installation of The Beast. After that, he's off to Australia. It seems that he can now begin his international leg in the quest to visit the most forensic laboratories. Jeff is one of our closest colleagues and by all accounts a genius, though some would probably argue that his revolutionary ideas make him more of a kook—at least that's what an F.O.G. might say. But ideas are what drive the wave of change, and without them, things become stagnant. Jeff and his ideas remind us a lot of the ubiquitous PC versus Mac television commercials. Jeff, of course, is the Mac. We'll let you guess who the PCs are.

When the academy first began, we heard stories of forensic researchers who were interested in developing a device that could record past sounds from a crime scene well after the crime had occurred. We have no idea how such a creation would work, but they were seeking funding for it. Sounds crazy, doesn't it? But then, maybe it's not as crazy as it seems. Who could have forecasted the advent of DNA, and the technology to analyze it, a mere twenty years ago? At one time, the fingerprint brush was the most advanced tool an investigator had at his disposal. And now look where technology is today and where it is headed for tomorrow.

Many things that we take for granted were discovered by accident, by sheer happenstance. Alexander Fleming wasn't looking for penicillin when his petri dish molded. Young Frankie Epperson just wanted a soda drink back in 1905, but forgot about it and left it on his back porch overnight, freezing the concoction solid. Eighteen years later, he remembered that childhood event and invented what some people claim to be one of the most important inventions of the twentieth century—the Popsicle.

Forensic science has not been without its research gaffes-turned-epiphanies either. The cyanoacrylate fuming process, better known as superglue-fuming, was accidentally discovered by the Japanese police when a fingerprint was inadvertently found on the underside of the lid of a jar of superglue. Ultraviolet (UV) photography, used by forensic investigators to detect old bruising beneath the skin invisible to the naked eye, was discovered by a police photographer who was just finishing off a roll of black-and-white film while he was taking pictures of a child.

You just never know where things may go or how things may turn out—serendipity can be a powerful forensic tool. Who knows what will be discovered in the future? Perhaps collecting of air samples at crime scenes and analyzing them for microscopic DNA particles, cologne, or some other piece of evidence that we cannot as of yet see with the naked eye or detect with the human nose. A large part of the current research funding is going to nanotechnology (science on the atomic and molecular scale). Eventually, that will probably be a reality one day too. But it doesn't really matter what *will* happen. The point is that a lot of technology exists *now* that can allow forensic science to be done faster and better and to be more of a vehicle in solving crime, not just in its prosecution. And it doesn't take a trip in a time-traveling DeLorean to realize that allowing it to go unused is a travesty.

Manifest Destiny

Lewis and Clark traveled four thousand round-trip miles on their journey to discover the American West. We traveled just over three times that many miles on our cross-country journey to discover the American CSI. Some may argue that Lewis and Clark had it much harder than we did, but that argument would be moot, particularly considering that Lewis and Clark never had to deal with the metal-detector-wielding officers of the Transportation Security Administration. Twenty lip balm confiscations later, our journey was complete.

Dozens of audiocassettes, hours of video recordings, and thousands of pieces of paper were collected every step along the way, all of which were used in writing this book. We encountered many more stories that we did not use—peripheral tales too fleeting to chase. Not to mention the other colorful characters who crossed our paths unexpectedly. Maybe those stories and characters can make it into another book. It's truly difficult to write about people and things that are in the present because nothing stays the same. Before all of the *i*'s were dotted and *t*'s crossed, things had already begun to change.

Texas Ranger John Martin retired from his Rangerdom and moved into the corporate world. In New Jersey, Sergeant Melissa DeFilippo was promoted to lieutenant; and in Tennessee, Lieutenant Jeff McCarter was promoted to captain. In Duluth, Sergeant Eric Rish was promoted to lieutenant and moved to patrol. Sheriff Bruce Montgomery of Sevier County, Tennessee, the man too ornery to give in to cancer, finally lost his battle. Even we have moved on to brighter pastures, leaving the academy behind. And New York CSI Sergeant Larry Walsh—well, he still loves his Spanish women. Some things never change.

In the end, all one can really hope for is to be a vehicle for change, and it became very apparent that we had done so in our time at the academy, even if just on a small level. We and the NFA clearly touched the lives of each of the real CSIs whom we visited on our trip across America. They approach their jobs differently, their departments think of them differently, and each one stood up and proudly said that more than anything else, he or she was more confident in working crime scenes. Confidence is a priceless thing and not something that can be gained overnight. And sometimes, having confidence is more important than having the latest forensic tool.

Overall, it was an amazing experience, our 13,500-mile odyssey of sorts, during which we were completely immersed in a world we had previously viewed only from the outside. It's a world not meant for most, no matter how much Hollywood continues to overglamorize it. Spending more than four hundred hours behind the yellow tape, with those hardworking men and women who pour their lives into their jobs, proved many things to us beyond a shadow of a doubt. For one, if many of the CSI wannabes could see and smell what we have seen and smelled, we are sure that applications into the forensic field would plummet. Second, no one can be a successful crime scene investigator if he or she acts as smug as that guy Horatio Caine on *CSI: Miami*. And finally, what stood out most was that no matter whether the killer says *y'all* or *ay'* or *howdy* or *yo*, if he says it in the cities and counties we visited, he'll be saying it from a ten-by-ten room, behind a cold set of steel bars.

GLOSSARY OF FORENSIC TERMS

AFIS is the Automated Fingerprint Identification System used to match found fingerprints with a database of known prints.

The **area of convergence** is the area in three-dimensional space where the violence or bloodshed took place. To determine the area of convergence, an investigator must first determine the angles of impact of significant stains using trigonometry.

Bluestar is a chemical used to detect blood. Crime scene investigators typically use it to detect cleaned-up blood at a crime scene. A unique characteristic of Bluestar is that it will fluoresce at the presence of blood in the daylight.

CODIS, the Combined DNA Index System, is the Federal Bureau of Investigation's software database of criminal DNA profiles. The database contains local, state, and national profiles of convicted persons, missing persons, and other evidence from unsolved cases.

Crime scene mapping is the technique investigators use to sketch a crime scene. Crime scene mapping can be done by hand by measuring the crime scene and drawing it on graph paper, or it can be done on a computer with mapping software.

Dental stone is a gypsum-based powder that is mixed with water and used as a casting material. The most common use of dental stone in crime scene work is in casting footwear impressions.

Dye stain is a chemical used to enhance cyanoacrylate-fumed (superglue-fumed) latent prints. The dye stain is fluorescent and used in conjunction with a forensic light source. Common dye stains are Ardrox and Basic Yellow.

Epithelial cells make up the outermost layer of skin cells, which are typically found in latent fingerprints. Latent prints are made by the deposition of the fats and oils found in the skin.

A **forensic light source (FLS)** is also known as an *alternate light source (ALS)*. The FLS is a lamp, either fixed or portable, that contains the UV, visible, and infrared light spectrums. The FLS can be tuned to specific settings depending on the item that is being examined.

Liquid glove is the generic term for an antibacterial skin protectant that, when put on the skin and allowed to dry, acts as a barrier against germs for several hours. Narcotics officers have been known to use this product to protect themselves from the germs commonly found on illegal drugs.

Lividity, also known as *livor mortis*, is the postmortem pooling of blood within the body due to gravity that causes skin discoloration. This discoloration can indicate what position a body was in, and for how long, after death.

Luminol is a chemical used to detect the presence of blood. It will fluoresce when blood is detected. Crime scene investigators typically use it to detect blood that has been cleaned up at a scene. As opposed to Bluestar, luminol will fluoresce only in complete darkness.

A **mitochondrial DNA profile** can determine the maternal inheritance from a DNA sample. Because mitochondrial DNA is passed through the mother's DNA to her offspring, this type of profile can identify mothers, offspring, and siblings. This technique is often used when a full DNA profile cannot be obtained, such as during hair analysis. If the root of the hair shaft is not available, then a mitochondrial DNA profile can be run on just the shaft of the hair.

Rehydrating a print is sometimes necessary when a cyanoacrylate-fumed (superglue-fumed) print needs to be made visible. When the fumed print is sprayed with a dye stain such as Ardrox, the print will fluoresce, making it more visible to the naked eye.

Ridge detail describes the specific, individual characteristics of a fingerprint.

Stringing a bloodstain is a method of visualizing how blood has spattered, using lengths of string to determine the area of convergence of bloodstains. A trained investigator determines how the blood traveled using mathematical equations to find the angle of impact. After the angle of impact has been calculated and the area of travel determined, a string is placed from the bloodstain to a fixed object. Typically, stringing is done on walls and floors.

Superglue-fuming is a method used by investigators to develop a latent fingerprint. Superglue, or cyanoacrylate, when heated to a certain temperature, begins to gas, or fume. When latent fingerprints are exposed to these fumes, the reaction causes the prints to turn white, thus making them more visible.

A **total station** is an instrument used by investigators to measure a crime scene. It measures angles and distances between two points.

ACKNOWLEDGMENTS

First and foremost, I'd like to thank my wonderful family. I'd like to thank my wife, Kolloia, for putting up with my sometimes insufferable moods. I know I wear you out. And to my daughters, Kaylie and Jetta, I want to thank you for putting up with my obsessing over your every move and know that you are and will always be Daddy's Little Girls. I love you all very much!

I'd also like to thank my parents, brother, uncle, and other relatives and friends for supporting me through all of my endeavors, and I'd like to thank my co-author, Amy Welch, for her friendship and hard work in seeing this project to completion.

J.J.H.

I would like to thank my amazing husband, Steve, once again for supporting me throughout the writing of this second book. You are amazing, and I couldn't have done it without you. I love you very much!

I want to tell my family that they rock! And I want to thank all of them for always supporting me. My parents, Garry and Sara Mick, are the best parents anyone could hope for. My big, little brother, Adam Mick, and my sister-in-law, Nicole, added to our family this past year in my perfect niece, Rylee, who will probably be reading by the time this book is published. And my nan, Minnie Arbaugh, asks me about the book every time I talk to her. I think she's more excited than I am. I also know that my papa, the late Don Arbaugh, is watching over me every step of the way. I love you guys so much!

I also want to thank all of my friends for supporting me throughout this process. And thanks to my co-author, Jarrett Hallcox, not only for having another good idea but also for your friendship throughout our crazy cross-country crime scene adventures.

A.M.W.

Special Thanks

It takes a village to write a book, and without that village, we would have been lost this time. First, we'd like to thank Berkley Books for taking on this project and to all of those who contributed to it becoming a reality. A special thanks goes to the president and publisher of Berkley, Leslie Gelbman, for her willingness to take on another one of our projects, and to our editor, Shannon Jamieson Vazquez, for persevering through to the end. We'd also like to thank our agent, Laurie Abkemier, from DeFiore and Company for being our sounding board and also our shrink.

We'd like to extend a special thanks to Patricia Cornwell for her gracious consideration in writing a foreword for our book. Her guidance and generosity over the years have been overwhelming and we owe her a debt of gratitude that we can never repay.

ACKNOWLEDGMENTS

And last, but not least, we'd like to thank all the men and women, and their respective agencies, who allowed us candid access not only to their departments and their work, but also to their lives. Each and every one of them, their names scattered throughout the pages of this book, took us in like wandering nomads, taking time from their busy work and family lives to provide us with an inside look into the real world of the CSI. We are very grateful for everything you guys did for us and are proud to call all of you our friends.

Jarrett and Amy